Embellished emotions for Scrapbookers

Adding Your Personal Touch to Poems, Quotes & Sayings

Only love can be divided endlessly and still not diminish

— Anne Morrow Lindbergh

I was so happy when Aysha was born, now I had the girl I always wanted and I loved her with my whole heart. Brett and I were thrilled when I became pregnant again with Alex and although I knew I'd love my new baby, I wondered how I could possibly love it as much as I loved Aysha. The moment Alex was born my question was answered, my heart had just grown bigger and I had an endless amount of love to give to both Aysha and Alex.

Elk Lake with Tia 8/03

Trudy Sigurdson

MEMORY MAKERS BOOKS

Denver, Colorado

Author & Artist	**Graphic Designers**	**Contributing Photographers**	**Copy Editor**
Trudy Sigurdson	Jordan Kinney, Robin Rozum	Camillo DiLizia, Jennifer Reeves	Dena Twinem
Managing Editor	**Art Acquisitions Editor**	**Production Coordinator**	**Contributing Artists**
MaryJo Regier	Janetta Abucejo Wieneke	Matthew Wagner	Sandra Ash, Karen Cobb
Editor	**Craft Editor**	**Administrative Assistant**	**Hair & Makeup Artist**
Amy Glander	Jodi Amidei	Karen Cain	Trisha McCarty-Luedke
Art Director	**Photographer**	**Editorial Support**	**Hand Model**
Nick Nyffeler	Ken Trujillo	Emily Curry Hitchingham	Darlene D'Agostino

Published by Memory Makers Books, an imprint of F+W Publications, Inc.

12365 Huron Street, Suite 500, Denver, CO 80234

Phone 1-800-254-9124

First edition. Printed in the United States of America.

10 09 08 07 06   5 4 3 2 1

Library of Congress Cataloging-in-Publication Data

Sigurdson, Trudy, 1969-
  Embellished emotions for scrapbookers : adding your personal touch to poems, quotes
& sayings / Trudy Sigurdson.
    p. cm.
  ISBN-13: 978-1-892127-84-6
  ISBN-10: 1-892127-84-9
  1. Photograph albums. 2. Scrapbooks. 3. Emotions in art. I. Title.

TR501.S54 2006
745.593--dc22

2006044896

Distributed to trade and art markets by

F+W Publications, Inc.

4700 East Galbraith Road, Cincinnati, OH 45236

Phone (800) 289-0963

Distributed in Canada by

Fraser Direct

100 Armstrong Avenue

Georgetown, ON, Canada L7G 5S4

Tel: (905) 877-4411

Distributed in the U.K. and Europe by David & Charles

Brunel House, Newton Abbot, Devon, TQ12 4PU, England

Tel: (+44) 1626 323200,
Fax: (+44) 1626 323319

E-mail: mail@davidandcharles.co.uk

Distributed in Australia by Capricorn Link

P.O. Box 704, S. Windsor NSW, 2756 Australia

Tel: (02) 4577-3555

Memory Makers Books is the home of *Memory Makers*, the scrapbook magazine dedicated to educating and inspiring scrapbookers. To subscribe, or for more information, call (800) 366-6465. Visit us on the Internet at www.memorymakersmagazine.com.

Dedication

There are many people without whose love, patience and understanding this book would not have been possible. Thank you to my wonderful parents, I would not be where I am today if it weren't for your endless support—I love you both. To my precious children, Aysha and Alex, for putting up with my constant "just one more photo…" and for making many a dinner while I worked late into the night. You both are my inspiration (and pretty good cooks!). To all my friends, you know who you are, for putting up with the unreturned phone calls and e-mails while this crazy process consumed me. To Dianne Pauls, my high-school art teacher and the one who made a difference in my life by nurturing my love for art and creativity.

Thank you to Karen Cobb and Sandra Ash for your wonderful contributions to this book and in helping me carry out my vision. To the Memory Makers family who has given me opportunities I will be forever grateful for and in guiding me through this process to make this book the best it could possibly be. You have taught me so much.

Finally, I dedicate this book to the loving memory of Kristy Tolsma who although gone from our sight will forever be in our hearts.

Table of Contents

Introduction 6-7

Incorporating Poems,
Quotes & Sayings 8-11

Sketches 96-102

Supply Lists 103-107

Source Guide 108-109

Author & Contributing
Artists' Biographies 110

Index 111

Chapter One
12-33

Love

Family
Children
Parents
Heritage
Grandparents

Chapter Two
34-55

Cherish

Spouse   Child   Friend   Pets

Discover

Chapter Three
56-73

Nature   The Beach   Winter   Spring   Summer   Autumn

Imagine

Chapter Four
74-95

Dreams
Inner strength
Happiness
Adversity
Destiny

The beauty of **family** brings us **cherished memories** we wish to hold **forever** For it is through our **memories** that our **HEARTS** find their way **home**

It all started with this one little border…well, the concept for this book that is. It actually all began about a year before that when I started making and teaching what was then dubbed as the "quote border" at a local scrapbook store. People seemed to love the idea, and it turned into my most popular series of classes.

Then in early 2004 while trying to brainstorm new class ideas for the upcoming year of Camp Memory Makers, I decided to try offering a "quote border" class, which was eventually named "Embellished Emotions" and featured the border shown on the left. I was overwhelmed by the response, and at the end of each class, I was always asked where more ideas could be found and…did I have a book? So when I approached Memory Makers about writing a book, this topic seemed like the perfect choice.

The idea of communicating emotion on a scrapbook page is a very natural one for me; after all, I started scrapbooking because I love photographs and the process of expressing myself through creativity. I classify myself as an "emotional scrapbooker" and consider my scrapbooks to be less of a documentary of my life, but more of a visual expression of my love for my children, family and friends. They will always have something tangible that reinforces just how much I love them, and the foundation of this is the photographs from throughout our lives.

So whether you embellish your own words or let others do the talking for you by using some of the many wonderful quotes and sayings out there, expressing what you feel in your heart will add richness to your pages unlike anything else.

So go ahead and get emotional, your family will love you for it.

Trudy

Trudy Sigurdson

Author and Artitst
Embellished Emotions for Scrapbookers

A dream is just a dream

A

goal is a dream with a plan and a

deadline

— Harvey Mackay

Incorporating poems, quotes and sayings

Incorporating poems, quotes and sayings is a wonderful way to add heartfelt emotion to your scrapbook pages, and using them to create word art on borders or pages will also add unique design elements and variety to your albums. You will be able to successfully create many wonderful pieces of art by following this basic formula as we go through the design process of the border to the left.

1) Finding the perfect verse

You may have your own wonderful words that you want to express in word art, but if you are like me, you may prefer to turn to other sources of quotes and poems that are available. There are many wonderful books that contain collections of quotes that will aid you in finding the perfect verse; a favorite of mine is the "Quote Unquote" series published by Autumn Leaves.

Many online scrapbooking sites have areas on their sites that are dedicated to poems and quotes. You can find some great ones at the following places:

www.twopeasinabucket.com
(click on "Resources" then "Pea Soup")

www.dmarie.com
(click on "Inspirations" then "Poem Place")

You will want to look for shorter poems that are just a few sentences long as these will be easier to break down during the sketching process. On the border to the left, you will see that I chose the following as my verse. Not only did I really like the sentiment, but also it was the perfect length.

A dream is just a dream.
A goal is a dream with a plan
And a deadline.
- Harvey Mackay

There is also an abundance of Web sites where you can go to find just the right poem or verse. Some of my favorite sites are:

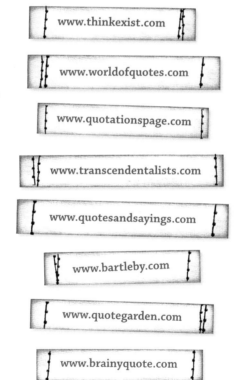

www.thinkexist.com

www.worldofquotes.com

www.quotationspage.com

www.transcendentalists.com

www.quotesandsayings.com

www.bartleby.com

www.quotegarden.com

www.brainyquote.com

2) Sketching out your design

You might not usually begin your layouts by sketching them out first, but rather by allowing your design to evolve as you go along. However, in this instance you will find it beneficial to preplan your word art by drawing a sketch. You can do this with a pencil and paper or on your computer, whichever you find easier. But since the next step in this process involves designing on the computer, you need to know exactly how much space you will need for all of the elements. See pages 96-102 for a sampling of some of the sketches I used when making some of the artwork in this book. Use these sketches to reproduce some of the projects shown, combine elements from multiple sketches to create something new or use them to inspire you when drawing up your own designs.

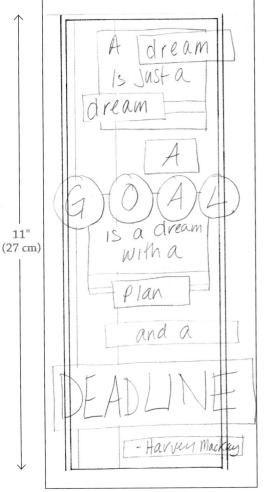

Notice that sketching is not fancy or complex, just a means of getting ideas from my head onto paper.

11" (27 cm)

← 4" (10 cm) →

{STEP 1} Start by drawing a border the same size you want your finished border to be (the one shown here and the majority of the ones in this book are 4 x 11" [10 cm x 27 cm]).

{STEP 2} Read the poem either aloud or in your mind to feel the natural flow of the words and to determine where the natural breaks are. These breaks will be the easiest way to split up your poem into different sections of text. Map out these sections on your sketch.

{STEP 3} Decide which words in each section of text are the ones you would like to highlight. For this border, I chose to focus on *dream*, *goal*, *plan* and *deadline*.

{STEP 4} Add the text to your sketch, making sure to highlight your focal words in separate boxes. You may also want to use different methods to create your focal words. Combining different computer fonts, stamps, stickers, die-cuts or other mixed media letters will give your word art more personality. On the sample border, I used a computer font for the bulk of my text, letter stamps for *dream* and *plan* and die-cut letters for *goal* and *deadline*.

3) Computer design

Now that you have a basic "blueprint" of your border, you can start to reproduce your sketch and its various elements on the computer.

{STEP 1} Open your word processing program and create a text box that is the same size as your finished border. For this border I sized it 4 x 11" (10 cm x 27 cm).

{STEP 2} Create separate text boxes for each of your main blocks of text drawn on your sketch and move them into place on your "border" text box. (I create separate text boxes for each section of verse and focal words so that I can position them exactly where I want them.) Add the general pieces of text to these blocks.

{STEP 3} Create additional text boxes that will feature your highlighted words and move them into place on your border. You will want to do this even if you are not using computer-generated fonts for these words as this will help with your spacing.

{STEP 4} Now that you have your design and complete verse mapped out on the computer, print out a copy on scrap paper. I find that in doing this I can better evaluate whether I am happy with my sizing and spacing of the elements. Make any adjustments needed and print again for a second look.

{STEP 5} Once you are completely happy with your design, remove from your computer sketch any words that will not be computer-generated. Print out the portions of verse onto cardstock.

4) Putting it all together

Now you are ready for the fun part of assembling and embellishing your project. Here are some tips to help you through the process.

Have your original sketch and computer printout in front of you as you create your border. It will help you assemble your project if you refer to them often as you have all of your sizing and spacing already figured out and shown here.

Note how I have some sort of vertical line on every border. The text blocks and focal words give the borders a strong horizontal line; by adding a vertical strip to the background, it helps give a better sense of balance. Try using different patterned papers, cardstocks, ribbon, lace, mesh, burlap or fabrics.

Don't forget to have fun! This is where you get to play by adding little bits here and there until your word art is full of personality!

Having elements extend beyond the edges of your border will give a more relaxed and less confined feel to your project.

Using different colors and adding dimension to your focal words will also help them stand apart from the rest of your verse and give them more personality.

Our most treasured family heirlooms

12/02

are our sweet

fAMILY

memories

- unknown

Chapter One
Love

"The Family. We are a strange little band of characters trudging through life sharing diseases and toothpaste, coveting one another's desserts, hiding shampoo, borrowing money, locking each other out of our rooms, inflicting pain and kissing to heal it in the same instant, loving, laughing, defending and trying to figure out the common thread that bound us all together." – Erma Bombeck

I have always loved this Erma Bombeck quote...maybe it hits a little too close to home? Although we have certainly had our share of ups and downs, the one thing I know for sure is that I would not be where I am today if it were not for the love of my family. Even though every family is as unique as the individuals who belong to it, we are ultimately all the same because we are connected by the love we have for one another. In this chapter, we will explore some of the different roles people play in our families and how to creatively celebrate our love for them throughout the pages of our scrapbooks.

Family: 14-17

Children: 18-23

Parents & Motherhood: 24-27

Past Generations & Heritage: 28-30

Grandparents: 31-33

Use alphabet playing cards to highlight words

For this fun and funky border, I trimmed the playing cards down to a workable size, shaded the edges with black chalk ink along each side and matted on teal cardstock. Notice how the chipboard heart works perfectly as a replacement for the letter "V" in the word "Love." This gives the word extra attention and charm while providing the border a stronger sense of balance. Mini rose page pebbles pull everything together by adding additional color and reinforcing the paper's circular design.

If you only have ONE smile in you Give it to the People you LOVE

— Maya Angelou

Let us be grateful to people who make us happy They are the charming GARDENERS who make our souls BLOSSOM

It's not often that we all get together, especially since Steve lives on the mainland, but since Mum won this trip, we all got to go to Disneyworld and spend a week of quality time together and take a long over due family photo! November 2004

— Marcel Proust

Combine different products

Create a page with word art as unique as the family members it showcases. Here I combined a variety of products to create a "flea market" feel where the viewer can look many times and still find something new. Note that even though the quote takes up the majority of the real estate on the page, there is still plenty of room to include journaling on a distressed shipping tag.

charming

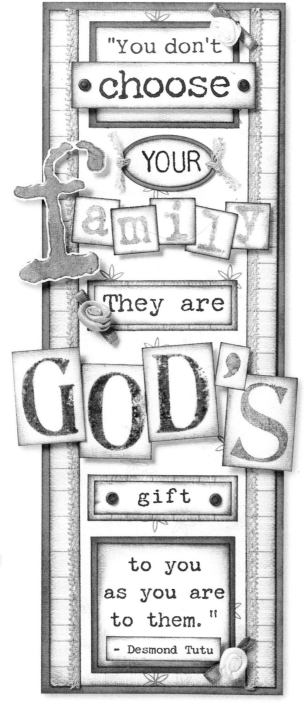

1 Stamp letter onto cream linen textured cardstock with vintage stamping ink.

2 Apply a layer of dimensional glaze to the stamped image and allow to dry on a flat surface. This may take several hours depending upon how thick you apply the glaze.

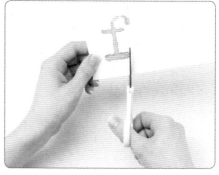

3 Once the glaze is completely dry, trim your letter leaving a thin cream border around the edge. Attach foam tape to the back of the letter and adhere to the border.

Make words shine

Deciding which words to highlight on this border was easy, and I gave them extra attention by adding a layer of dimensional glaze to the text (see step-by-step instructions). On this particular border, I combined five different fonts to add variety, but I made sure each font had a similar style so that nothing looks out of place. Notice how I cut my striped papers so they run horizontally on the border to help balance the strong vertical line of the border itself.

A Little Girl

is one of the most *beautiful* miracles of life.

— unknown

7/01/01

Find inspiration in everyday moments

Sometimes a photo of an "everyday moment" can be hard to scrapbook since there is often little to no story behind the photograph, as was the case with this one. My writing "It was a hot summer day so I took the kids to the park to play, and Aysha decided to have a drink at the water fountain" may be the truth, but it is not very interesting and doesn't do the picture any justice. By adding a quote, this photo now has much more of an emotional impact than if I had just told the facts of the event, and it makes the viewer linger on the page just a little bit longer. Also, adding writing on the chipboard heart ensures that the important information is included without upsetting the balance of the design.

The **family** is one of

nature's masterpieces

— George Satatayar

Experiment with horizontal formats

Creating a quote border as a horizontal piece of art can also serve the purpose of a title while still evoking the emotion that you are seeking for your page. On this border, the soft pastel colors and delicate wispy cheesecloth give the feeling of warmth and nurturing, perfect for a family layout. Notice how I gave a different look to the border and flower stickers by sanding them, exposing the white core underneath. Adding a light dusting of baby powder to the back of the flower stickers also allowed me to have them overhang the edge of the border without the worry of them sticking to other elements underneath, which would lose the light, wispy feeling I was seeking.

"Joy is not in **things,** it's in us."

— Richard Wagner

Use tags as word art

Tags are a great design element that help fill up an empty space on your layout, and including a quote or poem on one is an easy way to add additional emotion in a more discrete way. For this tag, I wanted my word art to be more on the subtle side, so I enlarged the point size of my font on just one of the words. This helps me emphasize my point, but also allows me to maintain the delicate balance created by the rest of the tag's design. Also note how I pulled the sparkle in the ribbon to the lower portion of the tag by adding shimmery beads to the center of my flower, giving it a bit more detail and personality.

Embellish chipboard letters

This baby tag will create a big impact on any scrapbook page and can be easily made from items you will likely already have in your stash of scrapbook supplies. I love the appearance of the chipboard lowercase "b," and I was able to easily embellish it by adding a simple silver heart charm attached to some beautiful ribbon. I also found a fabric tab in the perfect color, but its theme wasn't suitable for this project. I altered it by adding a rub-on letter "A" to some cardstock and adhering it to the tab. I was then able to incorporate it into part of the verse where it worked perfectly.

Mix up fonts

My selection of fonts on this tag reinforces the whimsical feeling of the verse. I decided to use a font with uneven placement to represent the chaotic feeling of "losing your mind." I paired it with a pale color scheme and cotton rickrack to soften the verse and give it a nurturing feel.

Tip from Trudy

Sometimes inking small elements like these letters can be tricky. Try holding your item with reverse-grip tweezers as you ink. You'll find it much easier, plus it will keep your fingers clean.

We are lucky to have many beautiful parks here in Victoria. The best with out question is Beacon Hill Park. Every spring the hills in the park that face Dallas Road are covered with a beautiful carpet of purple flowers. i'm not sure what they are, but i thought they would make the perfect background for some photographs of Aysha. i love these pictures of her and hope that she always remains as carefree as she was right here. Spring 2003

There is a garden in every
CHILDHOOD

An enchanted place where colors are
BRIGHTER

The air SOFTER

And the morning more
FRAGRANT
than ever again
– Elizabeth Lawrence

MEMORIES

Create word art directly on your layout

Not all word-art borders need to be separate pieces that you adhere to your layout; you can use your page as the foundation and build the border on top as shown here. After making a rough sketch of my page, I knew exactly where I was going to place my photos, journaling and title. The sketch served as the perfect blueprint for me to know how much space was left for my quote. I also created a visual connection between my border and the large photo by having elements such as my text and photo turns overlap onto each other, giving my page a more harmonious feel.

You don't raise **HERO'S**
You raise sons.
And if you treat them like **SONS** they'll turn out to be **HERO'S** even if it's just in your own eyes.
- Walter Schirra Sr.

hope

ALEX AT SATURNA ISLAND JUNE 2004

Find the perfect quote

I have always loved this quote by Walter Schirra Sr., and as soon as I saw this photo of my son, I knew it would fit perfectly onto my layout. The verse gives an emotional feeling with a sense of hope for the future to this "typical boy" photo of Alex playing with a stick in a puddle. The large, bold letters in my highlighted words help to balance the strong focal photo.

Tip from Trudy

I often find that when I am stamping on darker-colored cardstocks that my blacks are not as deep as I would like. To remedy this, I use a solvent inkpad such as Stäz-On by Tsukineko and my image is stamped in a true, deep black.

Adorn an album cover

Embellishing the cover of a mini book or journal with word art is a unique way to give it extra personality. Since the cover of this boy album featured a heavyweight cardstock with a white core, I sanded around the edges, framing it in white. A large chipboard circle covered in yellow paper makes a great dimensional mat for the verse, and additional blue circles reinforce the playful theme. I used oversized metal letters for the primary word in the verse and a monogram letter sticker and letter stamps to complete the look. Notice how instead of using the same style index tab on the side of the book, I used four different shapes to add to the album's youthful charm.

Verse: **Not Your Average Dictionary**

Use fibers as a border

Crafting a "rag" like border on your word art creates a unique and highly textural look. I further complemented this by using two different shades of blue ink on textured cardstock and matted inked cardstock to the underside of acrylic blocks to which I adhered my focal words. See sketch on page 96.

Tip from Trudy

When adhering cardstock to clear items such as acrylic or glass, make sure you have an even application of liquid adhesive with no air bubbles because the bubbles will be visible once the adhesive is dry.

Get sassy with die-cut letters

Sweet sentiment is given a playful
twist on this border through funky
die-cut letters and youthful patterned papers. This border came
together in a snap. I was able to successfully combine products from four
manufacturers whose products featured colors that perfectly matched
with each other. Combining two
different shades of blue distress ink
smudged on white textured cardstock
provides energy and visual interest
while soft green jewels add just the
right amount of sparkle.  See sketch
on page 97.

Machine-stitch papers to create your own background

Karen created an interesting foundation for her border by machine-stitching two
different patterned papers, opposite sides together, and flattening them out as if
she had sewn a seam on a garment. She then incorporated the white "opposite side
together" strip of paper as part of the background's pattern by adding distress ink
and soft green rickrack. Notice how she created a shadow for the word "When" by
cutting a second set of letters from dark chocolate-colored cardstock. Ribbon bows,
green buttons and colorful embroidered flowers are the perfect finishing touch to
this cheerful page embellishment.

by Karen

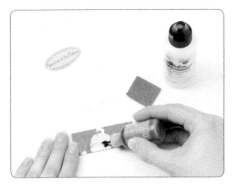

1 *Wipe slide with blending solution using a small piece of felt. Drop the first color of ink one drop at a time in two or three areas on the slide. Add two other colors, dripping in different areas of the slide and allowing time to dry between colors.*

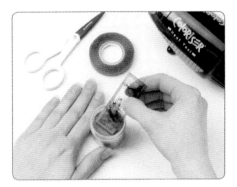

2 *Apply blending solution to a small piece of folded felt as you hold it with tweezers. Dab the slide where the colors meet to blend and create a mottled look. Allow to dry. (The inked side will be the back.) Apply ⅛" (.6 cm) wide double-sided tape along each edge on the front of your slide. Remove the backing and coat with silver embossing powder. Heat with an embossing gun to melt the powder.*

3 *Trim a piece of white cardstock to the same size as the slide and adhere to the back (inked side) with clear adhesive. Apply rub-on letters to the front.*

Have fun with color

The playfulness of carefree summer days is evident by Sandra's choice of colorful patterned papers and page embellishments. Notice the funky word blocks she created with glass slide mounts and alcohol inks (see step-by-step instructions). This is a fun and easy technique that provides endless possibilities. Sandra also added interest to her computer-generated blocks of verse by filling the background in orange, changing the font color to white and then printing on white cardstock. Handwritten journaling around the edge of her photo mat includes information without upsetting the balance of the page.

by Sandra

Time passes quickly when you are growing up. It seems like yesterday I was holding you in my arms admiring your cute little faces. You are now prepared to experience new dreams and create your own memories but always remember how much you are loved.

Unknown

1 *Remove the luster from the large button by sanding the button with sandpaper.*

2 *Use an old dryer sheet to apply a coat of olive green solvent ink to the sanded button.*

3 *Feed the silver threads through the buttons holes and adhere to the border. Attach the portion of verse to the center of the button with adhesive foam tape.*

Use less to say more

On this page designer Karen takes a more simplistic approach; although embellished and filled with technique, she chose to keep her visual elements to a minimum. A rub-on monogram applied to an inked chipboard circle makes a great center for a silk flower, while a distressed oversized button (see step-by-step instructions) makes an interesting frame for a piece of the verse. Karen also added dimensional glaze to her cardstock letter stickers, which provided just the right amount of shine to complement the shimmering silver threads, while a wire heart reinforces the feeling of love.

by Karen

A **Mother** holds her **children's** **hands** for a while... but their **Hearts** forever.

- unknown

Use dimension to highlight words

For this intermediate level border, I decided to highlight my focal words by using a different font from the rest of the verse and raising those words with dimensional foam tape. Because the border featured so much cream cardstock, it appeared somewhat neutral in tone. I easily spiced it up by incorporating green and cream striped ribbon, green flowers and rose-colored mini page pebbles.

Experiment with organic shapes

Sandra took a unique approach when creating a more embellished version of the same poem by shaping her border as a country heart. Using small patterned squares to create a quiltlike appearance is a great way to use up surplus papers in your craft room. Rows of stamped zigzag stitching, ribbons, silk flowers and vintage buttons give Sandra's border all the warmth of being wrapped in love.

by Sandra

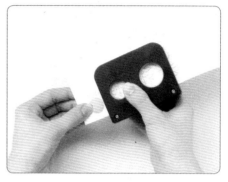

1 *Punch circles from patterned paper equal in size to the acrylic buttons.*

2 *Ink edges of circles with black chalk ink. Run circles through an adhesive-application machine so that the adhesive is applied to the patterned side of the circle.*

3 *Adhere the circle to the underside of the clear button and lightly ink the edges of the button. Add a letter sticker to the front of the button.*

Mat text in a variety of ways

Including words from your verse on cardstock index tabs is a great way to incorporate them on a word-art border, especially if you are having trouble fitting all of the words on your mats. After I secured the base of the index tab under a section of verse, I added a piece of foam tape underneath the top of the tab to give it extra dimension. Adding focal words on clear acrylic buttons (see step-by-step instructions) and a coordinating sticker tag help to complete the look that was embellished with flowery rub-ons.

Use paint to distress

I paid tribute to my mother by dedicating a special layout to the greatest role she has played in my life. Patterned or solid cardstocks with a white core are perfect to distress. Start by painting around the edges and, once dry, use an edge scraper to scuff the edges of your page. Avoid attaining an even appearance all the way around as this will look unnatural. Instead, try scuffing random sections of the perimeter by adding small scrapes, cuts and tears. This adds texture and dimension while adding little to no bulk on your page. You can also add a "shabby richness" to chipboard letters by adhering antique brads after you have painted and distressed the letters, while subtle heart charms and twill word snaps add additional charm.

Use chipboard letters to emphasize words

On this layout I highlighted what I felt was the most important word in the verse and used it as the title on a page about my dad. After sketching out my design, I knew exactly how many strips, and in what size, of patterned cardstock I needed to fit all of my words yet still allow me to include a large photograph and title. I inked the edges of each strip and used letter stickers to quickly complete the bulk of my design. Notice how I combined different sizes of the same letter sticker. This created more visual interest while providing me with enough of each letter needed to complete the verse. I also included important details by adding the "who and where" on the photo with rub-on letters. This is a great way to include additional information in a subtle way without affecting your initial design.

Every man
finds room
in his
FACE
for all his
Ancestors

Both of my grandparents were very involved with the Salvation Army, it is probably how they met when my grandpa moved to Paignton, Devon from Merthyr in Wales. This picture shows my great grandpa with five of his children and two of their spouses all dressed up in their Army uniform. Over the years it has been something I have seen my Nan wear on many an occasion. Front row, left to right - Peggy Roper (Tom's wife), Edith Evans (my grandmother), William F. Roper (my great grandfather), Olive Roper. Back row, left to right - Tom Roper, Idwal Evans (my grandfather), Leonard Roper and Leslie Roper.

Palace Avenue, Paignton, South Devon, England 1931

Ralph Waldo Emerson

Pay tribute to ancestors

Heritage layouts are the cornerstone of my family's scrapbooks, so I want to include sentiment on them even though I may not have known all of the faces that stare back at me. This page features a more subtle word-art border that utilized the last word from the verse as my handcut title, leaving me plenty of room to add important journaling. Strips of distressed patterned papers combined with dyed lace and doilies give this page a classic and timeless look.

Beautify word art with a border

A distressed molding strip makes an ornate border strip on this heritage word art. Apply one coat of chocolate-colored paint to the molding strip and wipe with a paper towel. The paint will remain in the creased areas while being wiped away on the embossed sections, giving the strip an aged look. Layer one side of the molding on a strip of dyed lace and cardstock and attach to your border. Combine shades of antique linen distress ink with charcoal chalk ink to give your pieces of verse a soft vintage look that is polished off with decorative rub-ons and silk flowers.

Create your own mats

Using distressed shipping tags as mats for text gave my word art a truly unique look. I began by dyeing the tags with walnut ink. Once dry, I heavily inked the edges with brown and followed with a lighter application of black. I then stamped the tags with random dingbat designs, added large ribbon bows and finally the text. I added mini walnut-colored page pebbles (available in a variety of shades) to the center of the taupe flowers to give them a more polished look fitting for a heritage album. See sketch on page 97.

1 Print text onto cream cardstock and trim word block.

2 Rub a light to medium shade of brown ink around outer edges of word block. Be sure to rub the inkpad at a horizontal angle across the cardstock's surface to ink more toward the center.

3 With a darker shade of brown pigment ink, pounce along the edges of your cardstock to achieve a darker, feathered edge. Start with a lighter shade of ink and finish with a darker one so that you don't transfer any of the dark ink to your light inkpad which could result in "muddy" colors.

Enrich a layout with flowers and fibers

My grandmother holds a special place in my heart, so it is only fitting that she has a special page in my family scrapbook. Sanding the edges of pattered paper provides a delicately distressed look that is complemented by leaving a thin cream edge to the handcut word "beautiful." Feathery flower petals are accented by rich fibers with iridescent strands that perfectly coordinate with the warm tones in the papers. Although the quote perfectly encapsulates the feelings in my heart, I also stamped sentimental text on the strip along the top of the page.

Create focal point with letter tiles

On this horizontal piece, a border of patterned papers combined with portions of verse, inked cardstock strips and funky rickrack complement the uneven tiles that highlight my focal words. Paper flowers with coordinating page pebble centers delicately embellish the corners and are given a sense of balance by having ribbon bows in opposing corners. Notice how I chose to have my darkest color be a shade of gray instead of black, which would be too harsh for this delicate color scheme.

Tip from Trudy

I love the look that can be achieved by distressing cardstock with ink. Combining different shades of ink can result in wonderfully aged elements.

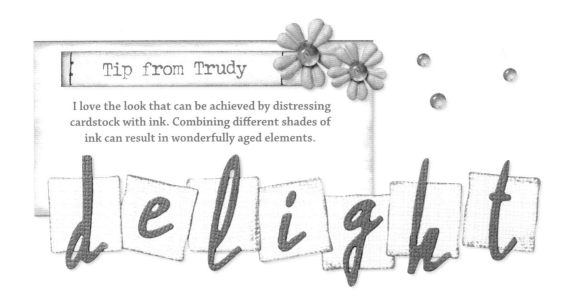

Mix up your letter stamps

This touching layout celebrates the close relationship between my children and their grandparents. After choosing the words I wanted to highlight, I decided to use a set of letter stamps that have the same font in a variety of sizes, allowing me to customize the size of my highlighted words to bring them just the right amount of attention. I created the word tiles by adding paper to chipboard tiles. I then sanded and inked the edges and stamped the words or letters in black ink. Finally I applied a layer of dimensional glaze and allowed them to dry.

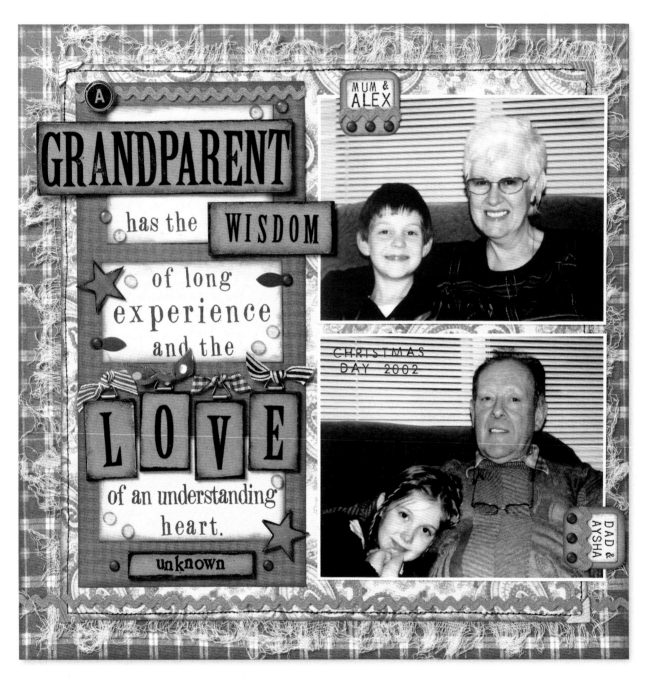

TREASURE

Some people, no matter how old they get, never loose their beauty

They merely move it from their faces into their hearts

— Martin Buxbaum

My Aunty Ollie has always been one of my favorite relatives and I am thankful that the kids were able to meet her before she passed away. She was a colourful character who had a unique and entertaining way about her which made you love her all the more. June 2002

remember

once upon a time

Beautify a layout with vintage pieces

Vintage-style layouts not only work perfectly for heritage photos but also for older generations in your family. For this page, I wanted to create a layout that reflects as much beauty as my great-aunt had in her heart. After I trimmed and layered strips of patterned papers, I found that the peach paper was too bright compared to the rest of the page. To remedy this, I applied a distressed tape measure rub-on to tone down the paper. Note the ornate photo turns that overlap the photograph. Although I wasn't lucky enough to have authentic vintage photo turns, I did have pewter findings intended for bracelets. I used wire cutters to remove one of the two loops on each finding and used the remaining loop to secure a brad through, leaving me with beautiful antique photo turns that add a subtle charm to my page.

08/08

TRUDY & DIANNE

Friendship

is a

knot

tied by

Angel's

hands

Chapter Two

Cherish

I'll be totally honest—I didn't start scrapbooking with the intent of preserving my photos in an archival-safe environment. For me it was all about the creative process and my emotional attachment to the people and places captured in my photographs (the photo preservation was just an added bonus!). I see my scrapbooks as illustrated journals, and I want to include all the different people in my life who share a special part of it. Some of these people will come and go as our paths only cross for a short time, while others will be with me forever. And then there are the four-legged kind who have managed to capture a little corner of my heart. Whatever its nature, I cherish each relationship because they all play an important part in my day-to-day happiness.

How did you meet your best friend? Was your spouse your high-school sweetheart? How does your relationship with each of your children differ, and how did that furry friend get to sleep at the foot of your bed? What is clearly in your memory now will gradually fade over time, but by creating these pages, your scrapbooks will be richer and have more depth as they celebrate these relationships within their covers.

Love for a spouse: 36–39

Love for a child: 40–43

Friends: 44–49

Pets: 50–55

Make a border shine with premade embellishments

Celebrate true love with rich colors, feminine accents and hints of metallic shimmer. Ink the edges of cardstock stickers, mat them onto cardstock and edge the mats with a copper pen. As I was creating this border, I wanted to have strips to place some of my verse on, but I didn't have any suitable paper or cardstock. To remedy this, I cut a cardstock sticker tag from the same sticker sheet into strips and added words from my verse with rub-ons. This gave me a nice subtle background for my strips that perfectly complements the rest of the border. Add a few other personal touches by adhering tiny jewels to the center of your flowers and as antennae on the butterfly. See sketch on page 97.

Create a romantic feel

This quote is perfect for a romantic page and could also work to express your feelings for many other people in your life whom you cherish. Create extra interest to your background paper by stamping paisley images with gray ink. Add a strip of layered ribbons to the left side of the border and complete with chalked and inked blocks of text. Notice how most of the text blocks have some form of added dimension raised with adhesive foam. Lace, ribbon and skeleton leaves support the romantic feel that is reinforced with word and heart charms, while strands of beaded wire complete the look. See sketch on page 98.

love
DOES'NT MAKE
the world go
'round
love
IS WHAT MAKES THE
RIDEWORTH WHILE
FRANKLIN P. JONES

s am & j on

IMPORTANT!

FOLLOW THESE EASY DI⋯

⋯EP BY ST⋯

Layer text over prepinted twill

This wonderfully romantic page is full of rich color and texture. Starting with cardstock as your foundation, attach your photograph in the desired location and add rows of coordinating ribbons. Adhere lace to the page with a few drops of liquid adhesive. Secure the ribbons with glue dots as liquid adhesive can leave residue marks on ribbon. Add words to flashcards and incorporate preprinted twill tape to serve as a perfect base for the sentimental verse.

Photo: Samantha Walker, Lehi, Utah

Embellish an album cover

Create a beautiful mini theme album to capture the essence of your relationship with a loved one. Covering a "naked" album like the one used here is easy by first removing the covers from the coil spine, cutting distressed patterned cardstocks to size and attaching them to the chipboard covers with a strong adhesive such as a spray adhesive. You can also add personality to the words in your verse by giving them each a different treatment. You might choose to color some with paint while others may call for paper to embellish. Pink wooden letters blend better with the other colors on the album after being given a coat of paint which was slightly wiped off, while easy-to-make typewriter letters (see step-by-step instructions) add an interesting touch.

CREATE TYPEWRITER LETTERS

1 Punch out circles from cardstock with a white core and sand edges.

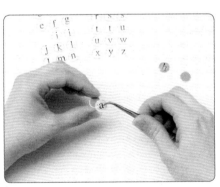

2 Adhere an epoxy letter sticker to the front of the sanded circle and attach an adhesive foam square to the back.

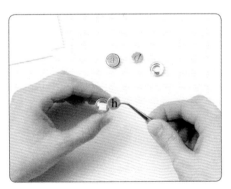

3 Remove the backing from the foam square and attach a washer (available from a local hardware store) to the back of the epoxy letter circle.

Combine computer fonts with rub-ons

A picture speaks a thousand words, but this sentimental quote really articulates the love this couple shares. To create the highlighted word blocks, adhere chipboard squares to the underside of patterned paper, ink the edges with distress ink and add the word with rub-ons. The remaining sections of verse can be created with computer fonts in evenly spaced blocks and added to the page to compose the border. The metal handles add a nice touch but were initially too lumpy to add to the page. My solution—hammer them flat! Well, not completely flat, just enough so that they are about as thick as the buttons and are easy to add to the page.

Tip from Trudy

When creating a page with a large photo and several strips of patterned paper, use a shade of cardstock from your stash you find unattractive or unsightly as your layout's foundation. Because the cardstock will be covered entirely, this a great way to use up sheets you would no longer use.

Create custom-made letter tiles

This vintage border would be the perfect touch on a layout celebrating the love between a couple in their golden years who have been together for a lifetime, or for a young couple just starting out. Horizontal borders are great for shorter verses as well as those where you want to stage the two focal words, as shown here, but you have to be sure that you give the strong horizontal lines a sense of balance. Use striped patterned paper at the top of the border and vertical letter stickers to help soften the horizontal lines. Paint chipboard rectangles black and lightly sand the edges to create the letter sticker tiles. Add the letter sticker and apply a layer of dimensional glaze.

Get creative with shapes

Who says all borders have to be rectangles? This one has additional charm by the very nature of its oval shape. To make the template for this border, I just opened up the word processing program on my computer, clicked on "insert" and then "picture" where I was able to open up the "new drawing" file and add an oval shape to my screen. After figuring out the size of oval I wanted, I added text boxes to the shape and typed the various pieces of text. I printed a "test" copy on scrap computer paper to check my sizing, and once I was happy with everything, I just printed it on the blue patterned paper and cut it out.

The best and most **beautiful** Things in the world cannot be seen or even **touched!** They must be felt with the **heart**

—Helen Keller

one little SMILE can fill a room with sunshine
unknown

Kara, Rachel and Jenna are so much fun to photograph because unlike Aysha and Alex, they like to have me take their picture. I had been promising Karen that I'd take pictures of the girls for her for ages... but I was always so busy and never got around to doing it. Finally after getting my new camera, it seemed like the perfect time. I was able to play around with my camera and managed to get some good shots of the girls.   August 21, 2005

Combine rubber letters with stamped text

The bright, cheery colors and patterned papers capture the playfulness of the three sisters in this charming layout. So often we just leave our photos in square or rectangular shapes, so adding curves to your photo is a great way to add variation to your pages (plus it's a great way to crop unwanted items from your photos). Adhere coordinating patterned papers to a solid piece of cardstock and add photos. Stamp text on paper and fabric tags and combine with rubber letters and printed text. Embellish with mini page pebbles, die-cut and silk flowers, ribbons and rickrack. See sketch on page 98.

Add emotional impact to an everyday moment

I love to take pictures of the everyday moments in our lives, but sometimes there is often not much in the way of a story to accompany it. This is the perfect time to add a poem or quote that will help enforce the emotions I feel when I look at these pictures. A strong, bold photograph needs strong, bold text to maintain a sense of balance, so I used big metal letters with clean lines for my focal words and printed the rest of my text on strips of blue distressed cardstock. Covering chipboard stars with coordinating patterned papers reinforces one of the focal words in my verse, but also adds interest in an otherwise minimally embellished but eye-pleasing layout.

Add visual punch with bold colors

These photos are from various "everyday" moments, so it makes sense to group several of them together on one layout and include sentimental word art. The colors in the patterned papers I used are very subtle, so I chose to add some contrast to the page by cutting my focal words out of a brighter, tangerine-colored cardstock. When making handcut titles similar to the one used here, be sure to cut out the center of the letters first (letters such as a, b, d, e, g, o) as the rest of the cardstock will help stabilize your letter. You can also easily cut the curves or tight corners in some letters by using various-sized hole punches. This will allow you to get in areas that are harder to reach with your scissors. See sketch on page 98.

Create your own background

Sandra created a soft feminine border with an interesting background
treatment. If you look closely you
will notice that she completely
covered her background patterned
papers with a layer of cheesecloth
sewn with freeform stitching. Portions of verse on colorful mats are
added on top of the cheesecloth and
embellished with silk flowers and
brads. The focal words are handcut
and chalked for extra emphasis. A
delicate, but visually strong, vintage
button border balances the horizontal lines making this a beautiful
addition to any page.

by Sandra

Go floral

On this border, Karen decided to play up the flowery theme of the patterned papers
by adding paper flowers, floral ribbon and flowers cut from her patterned papers.
She also had letter stickers that were a perfect color match to the papers, but the
style didn't necessarily match or fit the space she needed them to fit into. To solve
this, Karen cut around the edge of the stickers until she removed the unwanted
areas and now they fit perfectly onto her mini tags. She also wanted to use metal
letters that were a pewter color. Her problem? The other metal embellishments were
gold. Applying a coat of gold paint solved this so that they would work with the
other items on the border.

by Karen

MACHINE-STITCH LACE TO PATTERNED PAPER

1 Draw a diagonal line template on chip-board or cardstock and trim. Number each section so that you will know what order you will need to reassemble your strips.

2 Attach each template upside down to the back of your paper, trace and trim. Number each piece.

3 Adhere a strip of lace to the bottom of the back of each strip of patterned paper. Sew the strips to your page in numerical order by stitching along the top and bottom edges of the strips.

Print word art on transparency

I decided to take a different approach when creating the background for this page. I combined different patterned papers cut in angular strips and sewed them to my page along with layers of cotton lace (see step-by-step instructions). To create the word art, I first changed the computer screen to a landscape format. Next, I created several different text boxes for various words. With each word in a different box, I was easily able to change the point size of fonts and move them around the screen to position them in exactly the right spot. After I printed the quote on a transparency, I reprinted the focal words on white cardstock, cut them out and attached them onto the transparency with adhesive foam squares.

Make acrylic letters stand out

This border takes a sassy approach with playful patterned papers and clear acrylic letters. It's a good example of how you can successfully combine products from many different manufacturers while having them all look as if they were made to go together. Notice how different parts of the verse consist of different styles and colors of text. This conveys a more lighthearted feel that suits the rest of the border.

Use a portion of verse as a title

Sometimes you may have an unusual-sized photograph that makes adding other page elements a challenge. By incorporating a quote in the style of word art you can not only fill in those areas, but also have part of the verse double as your title. For my title I combined two different styles of chipboard letters that I covered with patterned papers and then sanded. The monogram "F" was further embellished by adding an additional paper strip studded with antique brads. I had also predetermined that the majority of my words were going to be stamped on strips of distressed cardstock, so adding one of my words sideways on an antiqued tag added extra interest, as did hanging some of the words by safety pins and string.

Print verse on strips

For this layout, I decided to make the strips of papers a fundamental part of my overall page design. I began by using an edge scraper and scuffing all four sides of the cardstock background. I then dry brushed around the edge with white paint. I trimmed four patterned paper strips, rounded the corners with a corner-rounder punch, sanded the edges and sewed in place. Notice how the photograph also has a cheesecloth mat. The frayed edges of the cheesecloth work perfectly with the scuffed edges of the page, as do the black letter stickers that without sanding would have been much too harsh for the soft feel of the page.

Place text on a circular element

When I started thinking about what to use on this page, certain things came to mind. Karen loves purple and flowers and has a clean, simple style. So this was a perfect direction to go when making a special page about her. Not only is the story of how we became friends recorded, but also the traits of her personality. Die-cut and rub-on letters comprise the fitting verse and were strategically placed on a large circle to catch the eye.

Quote: Tim Cahill

Choose colors and elements to reflect verse

Because of the very nature of the verse, I wanted to evoke a light, airy and angelic feel to this border. A soft color scheme, white lace and embossed cardstock help convey this feeling. I felt that black lettering would be too harsh for a delicate handcut title, so instead I chose to use a softer gray and followed suit with my choice of ink. A butterfly and dragonfly charm making a subtle reference to one of my highlighted words was the final addition needed to complete my border.

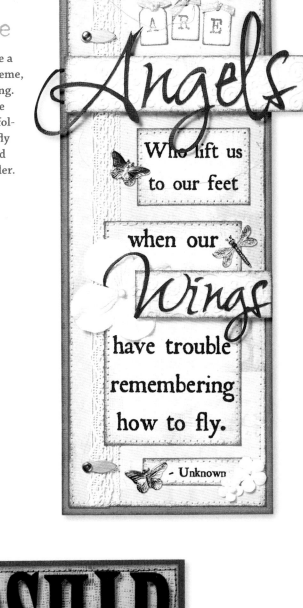

Add weight to key words

This border is a great example of how a quote can be used as a page title with the rest of the verse taking place as a subtitle. The 2" (5 cm) roman letter stamps were stamped onto dark chocolate cardstock with black solvent ink, trimmed, attached to the border with adhesive foam squares and covered with a layer of dimensional glaze. A 1" (2.5 cm) version of the same letter stamp was used to stamp "True" on a paper-covered chipboard tile and was also covered with glaze. Once dry, art hooks were added to the side and secured to the border with ribbon. Simple embellishments finish off this classic looking border.

Quote: David Tyson Gentry

Little Ted

Many people will walk in and out of your life. But only will leave footprints on your heart

— Eleanor Roosevelt

❤ true friends

Little Ted was not only my first friend, but my first true love. Grandma Wright bought him for Steve when he was born and he liked him, but his Gollywog was his favorite stuffie. Then when I came along, Mum put Little Ted in my crib and from that moment on he was MINE. Little Ted went everywhere with me and became quite the well traveled bear. When we moved to Canada my parents became good friends with the Guisti's and they had just had a baby girl. Now that I was "too old" to have teddies, I gave Little Ted to them. I was OK with this separation until I got older and I wish I had saved him. Then, at my wedding reception, Steve was giving a speech about my first true love and I knew exactly who he was talking about as he put his hand in a paper bag and pulled out Little Ted. Steve had managed to get him back from Joe and Maria who I had given him away to years ago. I was in absolute tears to be able to have him back again. So Little Ted stayed firmly in my posession until one day I gave him away again to another baby girl, but this time it was OK as it was my baby girl and Aysha now loves Little Ted (almost) as much as I do.

Journaling: October 14th 2005

Experiment with fabric letters

Who says that all of your friends have to be people? When I was little, my teddy bear was my best friend and a huge part of my childhood. So although it may at first seem a little odd, this makes it a perfect subject to record in my scrapbook and one that my children and grandchildren will love to read about. I decided to have a little fun with this title treatment by incorporating fabric letters on die-cut tags. The fabric adds a soft touch fitting with this subject about my lovable childhood toy.

my frIenDs

have made the story of my life.

– Helen Keller

Create a batik design on an album

A white cardstock-covered mini album provided the perfect canvas to create a batik-like design on the cover (see step-by-step instructions). After dyeing the cover and allowing it to dry, I added chipboard letters for the title and added the remaining sections of verse printed on cardstock. Self-adhesive jewels, rickrack and an abundance of colorful ribbons tied to the spine complete the look of this fun mini album.

1 Apply a low tack adhesive stencil to the front cover of the mini album. Apply one layer of dye.

2 Once dry, paint the inside areas of the stencil with another layer of dye to make the inside area darker. Add as many layers of dye until you have the shade you want. Be sure to allow each coat to dry completely before applying the next and before removing the stencil.

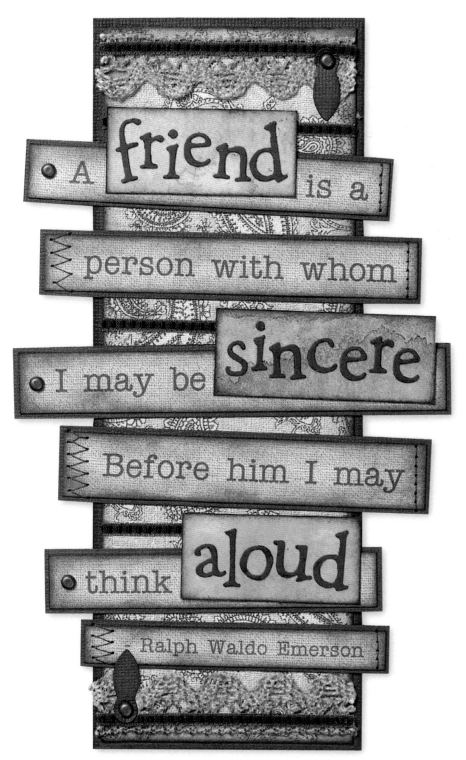

A friend is a person with whom I may be sincere Before him I may think aloud — Ralph Waldo Emerson

Tip from Trudy

If you dye an item and want to use it right away, lay it on several layers of paper towel and iron dry. Keep in mind that some of the dye will be absorbed into the paper towel and will result in a lighter shade.

Create a vintage look

This smaller border is the perfect size to use on a page in a mini album. I dyed the cotton lace in walnut ink and allowed it to dry. To keep the same antique look, I dipped the mats that feature the focal words in walnut ink and used distress ink on the remaining patterned papers and cardstocks.

Use burlap for a foundation

Take a more rustic approach in a border about your favorite four-legged friend. A frayed burlap mat sewn onto cardstock for stability is the perfect background for distressed letter tiles, a twill studded "collar" and distressed glossy tiles (see step-by-step instructions). Dip a metal-rimmed tag in walnut ink and then color the metal rim with a black permanent marker to better match the antique studs.

STAMP LETTERS TO CREATE WORD BLOCK

1 Glue chipboard tiles to the back of patterned paper or cardstock and trim to size. Ink the edges and toward the center with brown distress ink. Repeat the process around the edges using black.

2 Stamp letters with black ink.

3 Cover tile with a layer of dimensional glaze and allow to dry. If you are adding charms, buttons or beads, place the items in the wet glaze and they will dry in place.

Use chipboard as a base

Large chipboard shapes make great foundations for tags because they are sturdy and provide a little extra dimension. Here I layered two coordinating patterned papers and sanded the edges. Next I stitched around the edge of the tag and part of my verse with my sewing machine. Because I didn't want to hang my metal letters, I cut the loops off with wire cutters. Next I painted the letters with a chocolate-colored paint and lightly blotted them to create a more imperfect look. Ribbon was threaded through a metal buckle and attached where the two patterned papers join and then accented with a heart charm. The final step was to loop an additional piece of ribbon through the top of the letter "O" and staple to keep in place as a cute variation of adding ribbon to the top of the tag.

Quote: Martin Buxbaum

Tip from Trudy

Machine-sewing through chipboard is not as difficult as it may seem. Sew slowly to get the best results.

Employ circular shapes

Circles make a great variation from the traditional rectangular tag shape. Using a circle shape cutter, trim two circles that are about ¾" (2 cm) different in size from two coordinating patterned papers. Ink the edges of both and layer the smaller circle to the center of the larger one. Add the verse around the edge with rub-ons, stamps or mini die-cut letters. Mat, ink and add vintage lace to a strip of patterned paper and add a die-cut name (I added my dog's name), attach to the center of the tag. Cover an acrylic paw print charm with paint and wipe clean so that the paint only stays in the recessed areas. Attach a jump ring and hang from ribbon that is secured to the back of the tag to complete the cute addition to your page.

Quote: Susan Ariel Rainbow Kennedy

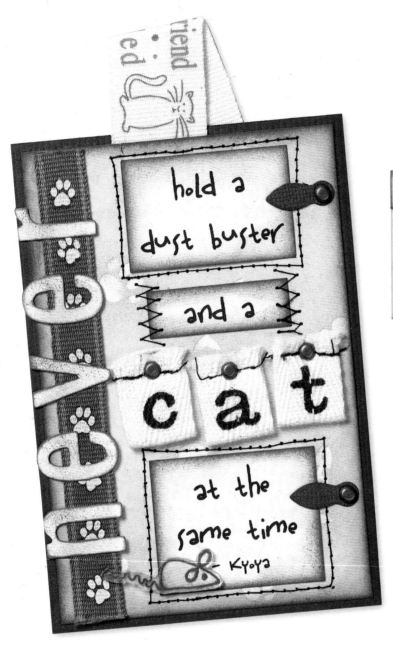

hold a

dust buster

and a

cat

at the

same time

— Kyoya

Tip from Trudy

Add visual interest to a tag by using two types of machine-stiching. A zigzag stitch and a straight line stitch complement each other well here.

Arrange text vertically

Add a bit of a twist to a tag by placing one of the focal words vertically along the side of the tag. Patterned papers with coordinating twill tapes and letter tabs complement the playful nature of the verse. A painted acrylic charm in the shape of a mouse adds personality, as does the casual stitching, paw prints and whimsical font.

cats

are intended to

teach

us that not everything in

nature

has a

function

Garrison Keillor

Moggie

I never thought I would ever have a cat. I'm a dog person, a 100% dog person, besides, I'm allergic to cats. So when we moved into our townhouse and were told we couldn't have a dog here, we were all very sad that Tia couldn't come with us, but grateful that Mum and Dad would let her live with them and we'd still see her all of the time. Then one night I was at a PAC meeting and Joanna said that she had some kittens that she was trying to find a home for. Hmm, a cat? But I'm not a cat person. So off we went to her house to look at the kittens, her very cute kittens, now I was in trouble. So Moggie came into our lives and I started to learn just how different cats were from dogs. Dogs don't jump on the fridge. Dogs don't jump on your head when you're sitting and watching TV or jump on the bathroom counter and chew your toothbrush. But how could you not love these things that ignore you all of the time and do nothing until it suits them. Don't get me wrong, I'm still a dog person, but I do love my cat. (Mogs at 5 yrs old - Oct 2005)

Use remnants to create new layouts

Because this layout consists mostly of photographs, I was able to use scrap patterned-papers for the remainder of available space. After I selected my photos, I laid them out on my cardstock foundation and decided how much room I'd need for my verse. Baby powder was applied to the back of black letter stickers to remove the adhesive, and dimensional foam squares were attached for additional interest. Hunter green paper was attached to the back of acrylic rectangles with letter stickers placed on top to highlight the focal words. These were then added to patterned-paper mats integrated throughout the sections of verse.

Tia is the sweetest dog anyone could ever hope to have and she brings so much joy and love into our lives. Christmas 2003

our

perfect

companions

never have fewer than

4 feet

Enlarge text for emphasis

A picture may speak a thousand words, but words can speak volumes, as does the verse on this layout about my dog, Tia. By printing the words of the verse in a large point size and changing the color of text to coordinating shades of blue and green, the words have become an important part of the overall page embellishment and design. However, when doing this you need to be sure that you have enough variation so that you keep things interesting. Notice how the word "our" was placed on tags, while "perfect" has a circular shape combined with a transparency (see step-by-step instructions). The other words were made from a variety of fonts, some of which were raised on dimensional foam squares. Once you have combined these various elements, the result is a wonderful layout showcasing your favorite four-legged friend.

1 Quote, 3 Variations

This quote by Sidonie Gabrielle Colette can be interpreted in many different ways as the following three samples demonstrate. Designer Karen Cobb and I both decided to make it relate to our dogs, while designer Sandra Ash made hers relate to her daughter's collection of stuffed animals.

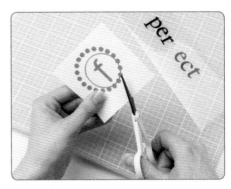

1 *Open up your word processing program and create two text boxes. In one text box, type the letter "f" in a circular font and increase the point size to about 200. In the second text box, type the word "perfect." Omit the letter "f" but keep the space open for where the letter would belong. Change the point size to about 85. Layer the two text blocks on top of each other to check your spacing. Once you are happy with everything, print out the circular letter onto white cardstock and trim with a circle template. Print out the "per ect" onto transparency.*

2 *Apply drops of liquid adhesive to the back of the letters on the transparency and center on the circular "f."*

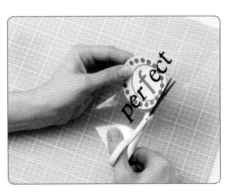

3 *Trim around the transparency letters and the cardstock circle. Add the acrylic flower with a colored brad to finish. Use adhesive foam squares under the circle to adhere to the page.*

Create a shape to reflect theme

Inspiration can strike at any time, and Karen was inspired by a dog treat when making this adorable border. After trimming a dog bone shape from patterned paper, Karen embossed "biscuit" along the center using a lettering template as a guide. Gently sanding across the letters helped define them and make them "pop." Karen hung the word "Our" as if it were a sign using wire wrapped over the top of the dog bone, and used twill tape around the bottom of the bone with the author's name hanging on a metal-rimmed tag to represent a dog's collar.

by Karen

Break verse into sections

Sandra went in a different direction and used the same verse to create a border with a cat theme. Sandra trimmed three rectangles from patterned paper and adhered them to her solid background. She added faux stitching around the edges with a rubber stamp and the various sections of the verse on tags, cut-outs and wooden tiles. Cat-shaped buttons and paper flowers add the perfect finishing touch to a border that would be a wonderful addition to any cat page. See sketch on page 99.

by Sandra

Each day is like a *snow flake.* A gift from *Heaven* with infinite *possibilities.*

WARM & COZY

snow softly falling

¡SS

snow bunny

– Lisa Hughes

Our one and only snowfall of the season. January 2005

Chapter Three

Discover

Spring, summer, autumn and winter—the four seasons. How completely different they are from each other but what beauty each one brings. I love spring for the first signs of new life and the beautiful colors of sweet-smelling flowers. I love summer for the long lazy days and warmth I feel on my skin. I love autumn for the crunching sounds of the rich red and burnt umber leaves that have fallen to the ground. Finally winter, my favorite of all the seasons. I love winter for the sounds it brings, the drumming of rain on my roof, the howling of the wind against my windows and the picturesque silence of a snowfall.

Most of our scrapbooks are filled with the faces of those we love, but not so often the sights and sounds of the seasons and the beauty in the world around us. This chapter will explore the ways we discover and take part in the natural splendor of our surroundings and the creative ways we can include them in our scrapbooks.

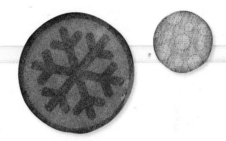

- Nature: 58–59, 72–73
- Winter: 60–61
- The beach: 62–63
- Spring: 64–67
- Summer: 68–69
- Autumn: 70–71

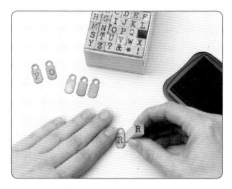

1 Dip mini jewelry tags in walnut ink and set aside to dry. Stamp each tag with a letter of the focal word. Ink around edges with distress ink if necessary.

2 Wrap the bottom of the text block with twine and tie a knot at the front. Add mini tags on top of the twine and secure each tag with an antique mini brad.

3 Cut three 2" (5 cm) lengths of ribbon, fold into a "V" shape and secure with a glue dot. Add the ribbons to the back of the word "Remove" and attach it to the top of the verse with dimensional foam tape.

Use a stellar photo as a background

Sometimes the best way to capture the stunning beauty of nature is with a large photograph. Because of all of the textures in my photo, I wanted to be sure that my border was also highly textural and had a "back to nature" feel. A handmade paper background and a burlap border combined with strips of twill tape, metal accents and twine help convey this feeling. Notice the different treatment for each section of verse (see step-by-step instructions). All the focal words are on separate pieces from the rest of the verse and were raised in some way. By distressing these blocks with chalks and ink, I was able to tone down the original color of cardstock which resulted in the perfect match for an outdoor layout. See sketch on page 99.

Be inspired by objects in nature

Celebrate warm, sunny days with a playful sun-shaped page embellishment. Use a plate as a circle template and trace onto two different patterns of papers. Tear out each half circle and tear again into strips. Layer the strips onto a cardstock base and stitch each section to the cardstock. Add die-cut letters to create your verse and apply a layer of dimensional glaze to the focal words. Finish off with torn cardstock triangles and strips of rickrack for the sun's rays.

Quote: Henry Ward Beecher

Create a design using everyday objects

Inspiration can come from the strangest places, as is the case with this border that was inspired by the way my son laid out three credit cards on my kitchen table. Three rectangles were cut from two different patterned papers, their corners clipped with a corner-rounding punch and then inked with monochromatic green ink. The pieces of verse were printed onto white textured cardstock that were also inked with two monochromatic shades of blue and stitched to the "credit card"-patterned paper base. After cutting out flourishes from the same patterned paper, I found that they were too light and didn't stand out enough against the background. Blotting them with monochromatic green ink added just enough color to help them "pop" off the background and complete the look of the border.

Crumple paper to mimic theme

Re-create the shimmering look of moonlight on fresh fallen snow by using silver rickrack, organza ribbons and crystal beads. To mimic the gentle unevenness of fallen snow, I scrunched the background cardstock of my border. The best way to achieve the perfect scrunched cardstock is to first spray one side with water and scrunch into a ball similar in size to a tennis ball. Carefully unfold the cardstock, check even distribution of wrinkles and scrunch again if necessary. (If you find you need to re-spray your cardstock, be sure to do it on the same side as before). Once you are happy with the wrinkles, flatten the cardstock and iron to smooth and dry. If you look closely you will notice that the two sides have a different appearance due to one side getting wet and the other staying dry. I tend to use the smoother, dry side on my layouts. See sketch on page 99.

Crop photo to mimic theme

Julia stepped outside one snowy afternoon to find her husband and daughter trying to catch snowflakes in their mouths. Luckily she was able to quickly snap an adorable candid photo of this father/daughter moment. Trimming the photograph in a circular shape helps reinforce the playful nature of the picture and gives the feeling of a falling snowflake while still allowing room for an additional picture. The quote was integrated into the title and decorated with clear acrylic snowflakes, shining jewels and dimensional glaze.

Quote: Unknown

Photos: Julia Hayes, Victoria, British Columbia, Canada

Center focal words

When sitting down to create this layout, I found that I only had a few 3" (7.6 cm) and 4" (10 cm) scrap pieces of the papers I wanted to use and I was unable to get more as it was late and my local scrapbook store was closed. Still wanting to use those papers, I overcame the problem by choosing vertical photos and placing them side by side across a cardstock foundation. This took up the majority of space on my page and allowed me to trim the scrap pieces of patterned papers into horizontal strips and layer them above and below my photos. By highlighting the words "Christmas Tree" and centering them at the top of my page, I was able to break the remaining portions of verse into two equal sections and place them on either side of my title, descreetly fitting in the verse while still allowing enough room for journaling.

12/01

Never worry about the size of your **CHRISTMAS TREE** In the eyes of children they're all 30 feet tall

Larry Wilde

Each year the Empress Hotel downtown hosts "The Festival of Trees". Local businesses and organizations decorate Christmas trees which are displayed through out the hotel and conference center. After paying a dollar, you can vote on your favorite tree and all of the money goes to the Children's Hospital. This was the first year that the kids and I went to see them and we were amazed at how beautiful and different they were.

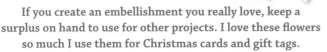

Tip from Trudy

If you create an embellishment you really love, keep a surplus on hand to use for other projects. I love these flowers so much I use them for Christmas cards and gift tags.

Arrange letters creatively

I decided to experiment with arranging my text in a unique way by running one of my focal words vertically down the side of this traditional Christmas border. Scrunched cream cardstock and sheer olive ribbon were sewn onto a red border to which I attached the letters with adhesive foam. To make the poinsettias, I punched two red and one olive flower with a large flower punch. Next the red flowers were layered on top of each other and two petals were cut from the olive flower and attached to the back of the red flower. After adhering small yellow beads to the centers and slightly bending up the top layer of petals (for additional dimension), my flowers were complete.

waves a *magic* wand over this world, and behold

CHRISTMAS

everything is softer and more *beautiful*

— Norman Vincent Peale

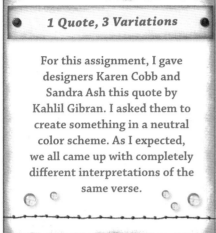

does the **song** of the sea end at the shore or in the **hearts** of those who **listen** to it?

Kahlil Gibran

Does the song of the

sea

end at the shore

or in the hearts of those who listen to it?

Kahlil Gibran

Alter embellishments to fit layout

Sandra decided to take a more simplistic approach when creating her border. After matting patterned paper on cardstock, she stamped her focal words onto patterned papers and cut them out. The remaining portion of verse was printed onto cardstock, and the edges were torn and inked with blue distress ink. Jute mesh was added down one side and the strip was then added to the border. Sandra found that she had sand dollar charms that would be perfect for the border if it weren't for the fact that they were gold. After covering them with a layer of white paint, they worked perfectly to finish off this calm and soothing page embellishment.

by Sandra

Create a custom foundation with unique items

All of the textures of the coast are captured in this unique border. Fish netting was cut to size for the base of the border while strips of muslin were dyed in walnut ink and hung to dry. Print the verse onto cardstock, tear into sections and dye with walnut ink. Once dry, stain the edges with a walnut ink dauber and sew onto the muslin. Stamp the word "sea" with a vintage typewriter letter stamp dipped in paint and trim. Stain the letters with the walnut ink dauber so that they look as equally distressed as the other page elements. Once all of the pieces are dry, attach them to the fish netting by tying on with twine or securing with jump rings and safety pins. Final touches of charms and shells complete the effect of treasures found washed up on the shore.

APPLY SAND TO FOCAL WORDS

1 Cut a 2 x 3" (5 cm x 7.6 cm) rectangle from a sheet of double-sided adhesive for each letter of the word "shore." Peel off the release paper and place the letter facedown onto the adhesive.

2 Place the release paper back on top of the metal letter and press down to make sure air bubbles are gone and your surface is flat. Remove the release paper and trim around the letter with a craft knife.

3 Remove the remaining piece of release paper and apply sand to the front (sticky side) of the letter.

I wonder why the waves gently glide towards the shore and back to sea leaving me new treasures to find. Other times they seem to be angry as the waves come crashing towards me trying to get my feet wet. Whatever the reason, I could listen to nature's wonders forever as the beach is my favorite place to be when the weather is nice.

Create rhythm through type

Karen's approach to her page was to make the quote the predominant embellishment; this resulted in a wonderful design that leads your eye around every inch of the layout. Look at the lines of the photograph and notice how her blue elements line up with the sky and ocean, whereas her neutral, sandlike items are grounded by the photograph's pebbled shore. Karen dyed cheesecloth in walnut ink and positioned it in the upper corner of her page and placed other elements on top as if they had been "caught" in a net. She created unique letter tiles for the word "song" by applying distressed rub-on letters to epoxy shell stickers and raising them with adhesive foam tape. Finally, she covered large metal letters with sand (see step-by-step instructions) to complete a page that has all the textures of the shore.

by Karen

Use fabric in place of paper

Although there is an endless supply of patterned papers geared to every theme a scrapbooker could dream of, fabric makes a nice alternative by adding softness and texture with little to no bulk. Trim a chipboard base and round the corners with a punch. Next attach torn strips of fabric with sticky lines of adhesive. Staple or attach mini brads to the ends of some of the fabric strips. After adding a handcut title and using die-cut letters for the remaining portions of verse, fold silk flowers in half and attach them to the edge of the mats with eyelets and ribbon. Small paper flowers, colorful ribbon and clear photo turns finish off this delightful spring border.

Quote: T.E. Brown

Get creative with double-sided paper

Convey the feeling of delicate spring flowers with feminine embellishments and a pastel color scheme. Patterned paper was sanded and attached to a cardstock mat, and because I used double-sided paper, a 1" (2.6 cm) strip of the paper's reverse side was sanded and added to the left side of the mat with a layer of lace placed on top. All of the text was printed on white cardstock with the focal words printed in a different font and larger point size for emphasis. The edges were also chalked in soft pink and attached to the border with dimensional foam tape, while the remaining strips of verse were left white and attached flat against the mat. A final touch of pale pink mini page pebbles is reminiscent of morning dewdrops fitting perfectly with the border's verse.

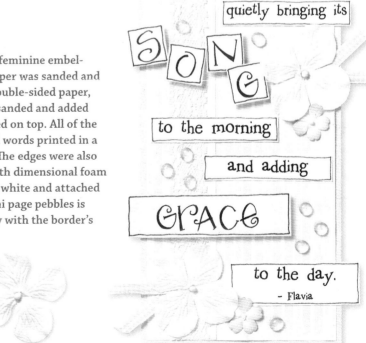

Each FLOWER is a voice of NATURE quietly bringing its SONG to the morning and adding GRACE to the day.
— Flavia

A Happy life is built up of little clumps of flowers noticed along the roadside

unknown

I have driven down the same road twice a day for several years taking the kids to and from school when one day I saw this little clump of poppies growing out from amongst the gravel against a telegraph pole. You don't see this kind of poppy very much over here so instantly I was a child again back in England. I remember playing in a field filled with red poppies. My friend Louise and I are popping the buds open and peeling apart the tightly wrapped petals before we moved onto the next one to do it again.... "I should photograph them," I think, but I never seem to have my camera with me. Again the next day I see the same little clump of poppies and have the same thoughts as I did the day before. "I have to take a picture of them before they're gone," I think. So this time before driving the kids to school I quickly grab my camera and throw it in the car. I didn't care if everyone else driving down the road was wondering what on earth I was doing taking photos of wild flowers because now I have my poppy photos and every time I look at them I am that 11 year old girl playing in a field of red poppies with her friend.

Spring 2002

Start with a sketch

You may have photos sitting in an album waiting for the day when inspiration strikes and you're ready to scrapbook them. That was the case with these pictures. I had taken them awhile ago but never did anything with them until I came across this quote and I knew they would be perfect for each other. Because I was using one large and two smaller photos, a large amount of space on my page was taken up. Sketching out my design before I started cutting any paper really helped me plan out how and where I was going to fit everything in. The result was a well-balanced page with enough room for multiple photos, a large journaling block and a decorative verse area. See page 100 for sketch.

NATURE

is the art of

GOD

Ralph Waldo Emerson

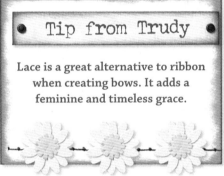

Tip from Trudy

Lace is a great alternative to ribbon when creating bows. It adds a feminine and timeless grace.

Beautify shorter quotes on tags

Celebrate the beauty of the world around us by incorporating sentiment on a tag. Layers of embossed papers and lace sewn onto the tag's base make a great foundation for the verse. I combined die-cut letters and matted text and embellished with iridescent flowers and shining jewels.

Create a tag from remnants

Making tags to embellish your pages is a great way to use up little bits of scrap papers. I found that I had three coordinating and similarly sized squares of patterned papers that would work perfectly for this project. After lightly inking the edges, I attached them to a larger piece of patterned paper and added die-cut letters for my focal words and printed the remaining verse on cardstock. I finished it off by adding delicate ribbon, lace and paper flowers. The result was a quick solution for making a tag with nice clean lines.

Quote: Countess of Blessington

Tip from Trudy

The design of this tag would also work well enlarged and used as a border down the side of a 12 x 12" (31 cm x 31 cm) page.

Use a frame as a foundation

A frosted acrylic frame made a great base for this cute page embellishment that came together in a snap. Layer the acrylic frame on white cardstock (this will help the colors "pop") and sew onto a pink cardstock mat. Use die-cut, rub-on or letter stickers to add your verse and position around a silk flower. Square brads and white twill tape finish off this whimsical look.

Quote: Ralph Waldo Emerson

Use journaling as a page border

The playful spirit of two preteen girls is evident in this carefree layout. After sketching the design of my page, I realized that I didn't have anywhere to put my journaling. I didn't want to alter the placement of my elements so I decided the best way to fit in the journaling was to incorporate it around the outside edges next to where I was planning on sewing a border. Strands of ribbons, additional stitching, funky flowers and the shimmer of jewels capture all things girly and helped to complete the page.

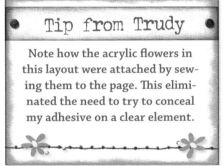

Tip from Trudy

Note how the acrylic flowers in this layout were attached by sewing them to the page. This eliminated the need to try to conceal my adhesive on a clear element.

Contrast bold tones with neutral tones

This fun border captures the feeling many of us have on those lazy summer days. Print the verse on two different shades of textured cardstock and heavily ink the edges. Layer strips of bright patterned papers onto a red cardstock mat and add the verse. Notice how I incorporated cream into my color scheme. This helps pull out the flowers in the patterned paper and soften the brightness of the reds and orange. A sprinkling of red beads and mini paper flowers pull the whole look together.

Quote: James Dent

Add shimmer with metallic letters

When I look at this border, my thoughts wander off to images of a summer night's sky illuminated by the setting sun. Golden yellows and rich reds are infused with iridescent purples that melt together. Metallic-colored acrylic and chipboard letters (see step-by-step instructions) work perfectly for the focal words, and black letter stickers help define the rest of the verse. Jewel-toned silk flowers are highlighted with amethyst rhinestones while clear photo turns and an acrylic circle received the same metallic treatment as the letters. Once all put together, the result is a beautiful addition to any page.

USE METALLIC LEAFING TO ADD SPARKLE TO CHIPBOARD LETTERS

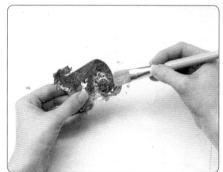

1 Apply an even layer of adhesive to the back of an acrylic letter. Cover the back (adhesive side) of the acrylic letter with flakes of metallic leafing. Rub your finger across the back to flatten and to make sure the flakes are properly adhered to the letter.

2 Brush off the excess flakes by rubbing the letter with a dry, stiff-bristled paintbrush.

3 Cover the front of the letter with chalk ink and be sure to fill in all of the recessed areas. Wipe away excess ink.

Layer type over a large photograph

Large photographs can have a stunning impact on scrapbook pages. Here I used the focal photo as part of the background for the right side of the layout. I experimented with my highlighted text by having it extend across the polka-dot patterned paper border onto the photo. I added a fun touch by connecting a distressed tag and the letter "u" with a piece of tied twine. See sketch on page 100.

The Heart of Autumn

must have broken here and poured it's Treasure out upon the leaves.

Charlotte Fiske Bates

Winter is an etching,

Spring a watercolor,

Summer an oil painting

& Autumn a mosaic of them all.

Divide design into quadrants

Dividing this border into four sections with each section representing one of the four seasons felt like a natural way for me to go when making this border. I chose patterned papers that I felt represented each of the seasons, which were then inked and sewn together on a darker brown background. Die-cut tags made the perfect mats for my focal words, and colorful ribbons added extra pizazz. The remaining verse was printed on lighter patterned paper, inked and sewn to the border and anchored with a photo turn to balance out the design. Smaller leaf-shaped die-cut tags layered and secured with a mini brad added that little something extra and finished off this more graphic-styled border.

Alter letters to match color scheme

Although the majority of the products I used on this border were all from one coordinating line, the rubber letters were lighter and brighter than what I wanted. An easy solution to fix this was to cover the letters with a layer of brown paint and wipe clean. The surface layer of paint was removed while leaving paint in the recessed areas, resulting in a darker letter, perfect for what I had in mind. A quick swipe with a brown inkpad also toned down the paper leaves, making them coordinate better with the remaining elements of the border.

Quote: Albert Camus

Make photos center stage

I'll be honest and admit that this page has a lot going on, but even though the background is full of little details, notice how your eyes are still immediately drawn to the photographs. All of the elements on the page are basically monochromatic which allows the vibrant color of the leaves against the contrast of my son's jacket to really jump off the page, plus the direct eye contact of this engaging photo draws you right in. So even though the background is filled with different elements, my photos are still the focal point. Try this technique yourself the next time you want to make a heavily embellished page. See sketch on page 100.

Use a monogram as a background

With monograms being so popular, I decided to create a funky monogram border with a fresh spring feel to it. I first enlarged a lowercase "d" on my computer screen to a 700 point size. I then flipped the letter backward (mirror image) and printed it onto scrap computer paper. This was attached to the back of chipboard with a temporary adhesive and trimmed to be the monogram letter. I then attached the letter to the back of patterned paper, trimmed it and sanded the edges. A piece of transparency was placed to the center of the "d," allowing me to attach "floating" die-cut letters. Finally, the entire letter was popped up with adhesive foam tape.

1 Quote, 3 Variations

For this next assignment, I asked designers Karen Cobb and Sandra Ash to use the quote "Delight in the beauty that surrounds you" (author unknown). Because this verse would also work well for other themes, they had to be sure to use it in relation to nature or one of the four seasons. I also asked them to use the color green as part of their color scheme.

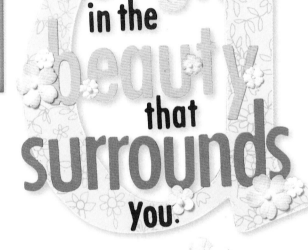

Trace patterns onto rub-ons

Because Karen usually scrapbooks in 8½ x 11" (21.6 cm x 27.9 cm) format, her smaller border is designed to fit perfectly with that space in mind. The patterned papers she chose to use had printed circles on them, which Karen wanted to emphasize, so she traced the circles onto the rub-on, cut them out and applied them to the circles on her paper. The letter stickers for the word "delight" were stuck on cardstock and trimmed using the edge of the clear sticker as a cutting guide. Delicate inking, ribbon and flowers finish her border that would be perfect for any fall-themed layout.

by Karen

STAMP DECORATIVE IMAGES ON CLAY TILES

1 *Roll out the clay until it's about ⅛" (.3 cm) thick. Ink the decorative square stamp with a clear inkpad and stamp into the clay. The ink will help keep the clay from sticking to the stamp.*

2 *Use a craft knife to trim around the stamped square. Bake clay according to product instructions and allow to cool.*

3 *Color the decorative tile first with green ink and then highlight with orange ink.*

Arrange photos like a mosaic

Sandra took an interesting approach when incorporating her photographs onto her layout. By placing them together in a mosaiclike format, she managed to fit six photos onto one single layout while giving the illusion of one large photograph. With her all-important journaling positioned under the photographs, Sandra had plenty of room to include the inspirational verse that makes you see her photos in a whole new light. Textured clay tiles (see step-by-step instructions) and satin flowers combined with vintage patterned papers finish off this layout about her uncle's love of nature.

by Sandra

Chapter Four

Imagine

Our lives are filled with milestones and various important or seasonal events. You can be sure that the scrapbooker in the family is standing there with a camera tightly within his or her grasp, waiting to capture each and every moment. But what about all of the other moments in between? The everyday moments? This is how and who we really are, the heart and soul of our lives.

I regard my albums as photographic journals to my children, a place they can always go to and read about my love, hopes and fears I have for them as they grow up. So scrapbooking with what I call "nothing photos" often means that you have little to no story behind a picture, hence not a whole lot to journal about. This is where adding poems and quotes really comes into play and gives these kinds of photos a whole new meaning. Everyone who picks up your album and looks through its pages will gain a better insight of you, your family and your love for each other as he or she flips through its pages and sees those all-important events. And more important, they'll see the heart and soul of your lives.

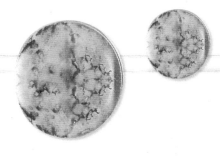

Dreams: 76–80

Inner strength: 80–83

Happiness: 84–89

Adversity: 90–91

Destiny: 92–95

1 *Choose a set of white-backed letter stickers to use for highlighted words. Remove the letters and attach to wax paper for later use on another project. Use a black pen to even out the black lines around the inside of the negative space left by the letter.*

2 *Print the photograph twice; set one print aside to use as the page background. Use the other to attach the negative-space letter outline. Be sure to place the letters in the correct order so that the colors will match up when you later attach them to the page.*

Use a photo as a background

I was on the plane flying home from teaching in Boston when I looked out the window; outside I saw the most beautiful sunset from the unique perspective above the clouds. The sky was filled with a stunning blend of blue to pink to purple back to blue, with a glimpse of the moon shining like a crystal in the sky and the plane's engines glowing with the setting sun. I was overwhelmed with how beautiful it looked. "Everyone should have the chance to see this," I thought. When I sat down to scrapbook the photo, I found that nothing did the picture or its colors justice. Once I decided that the photograph needed to be large and receive a simple treatment, everything else just fell into place. The negative outlines leftover from letter stickers and an additional copy of the photograph make for a subtle, but strong, title (see step-by-step instructions).

3 *Trim each letter, making sure to cut around the black outline. (Run along the edges of the cut letter with a black pen to even out if needed.) Attach dimensional foam adhesive to the back of each letter and adhere to the photograph set aside as the page background.*

Use ribbon to add a decorative touch

This inspirational message has been a longtime favorite of mine and would work well on a variety of page themes. Layers of patterned-paper strips create a soft background for matted blocks of text. Die-cut photo turns make great "loops" for stringing and tying ribbon when adhered to the backs of letters, as I did for the word "hope." Strips of sage cardstock add an extra touch of color to the text that would have otherwise been quite pale. Additional ribbon, matching buttons and extra brads finish off this motivational border. See sketch on page 101.

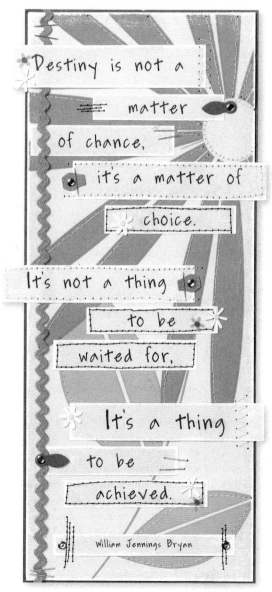

Stitch a flower

So many manufacturers have papers in their product lines that feature large, bold border prints. These papers can be great for word-art borders because the pattern section works well for the foundation and the remaining plain paper can be used for printing your text. After sanding the edges of the border paper, I stitched the outline of the flower for added interest and texture. The strips of text were printed on the plain portion of the paper, trimmed to size and then sanded along the edges. They were then added to the border either by different stitching treatments or staples. Olive rickrack, die-cut photo turns and tag toppers finished with mini flower embellishments complete the simple look of this border.

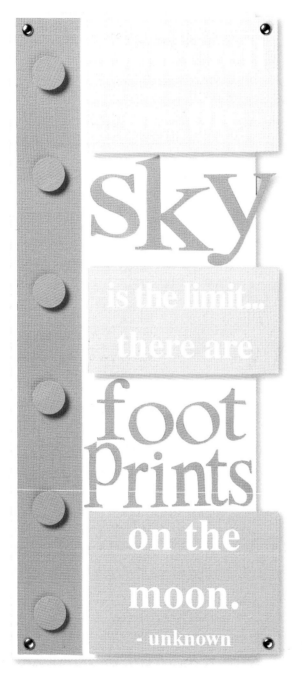

sky

is the limit...

there are

foot
Prints

on the

moon.

- unknown

Use type as your primary visual element

Although there are so many beautiful shades of monochromatic cardstocks available you may not always have what you need when you need it, or you may just want to custom make your papers. This border is made up entirely from white cardstock, which I printed on my computer in the various shades of blue. First start by making three text boxes and type in your text. Highlight the text and change the color to white. Next, highlight the text box and change the fill color to blue. I changed mine so that I would have light, medium and darker version of the same color. Secondly, type out your focal letters and change the color to the darker shade of blue. Lastly, create a larger text box and change the fill color to your darker blue shade. Print all of this out on white cardstock. Trim the text boxes, handcut the focal words and from the remaining solid blue text block, cut a border strip and punch out circles. The circles can be added to the solid border strip with dimensional foam squares.

Tip from Trudy

Don't be afraid to keep things simple by keeping accents or embellishments to a minimum. Sometimes the words themselves impart the most impact.

alex

Sometimes you may have a dream that you think is too far from your reach.

But it isn't. Nothing is. You can achieve anything that you set your

mind too and you can accomplish more than you know. You just have to try.

Alex taking the tender from Playa Del Carmen to Cozumel,

Mexico. March 2005 Explorer of the Seas

Always follow your

DREAMS

Even if you fall down

along the way – Unknown

dream

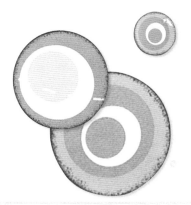

Add impact to non-action photos

These photos are a good example of what I referred to earlier as "nothing photos." My son was just sitting watching the waves while we were on a small boat and I quickly snapped a couple of shots of him. Because of this, there isn't really much of a story to tell. By adding an inspirational quote, the page now has much more meaning. The portions of verse were printed in the same manner as on the "Footprints on the Moon" border where I changed my text color to white and fill color to blue. I also created a solid blue text box and then placed a smaller text box with journaling inside it. This gave me the matching blue outline around each strip of journaling.

Add grace with organza, lace and ribbon

For this beautiful baby page, I cut random pieces of patterned paper and inked them with monochromatic gray ink, then layered and machine-stitched them to a cardstock foundation. Strips of shimmering organza, delicate lace and satin ribbon are combined with silk flowers to create a layout delicate enough for this adorable baby girl. The handcut cardstock title was originally the same color as the foundation cardstock but I found that it didn't stand out against the patterned papers as much as I wanted, so I blotted it with gray ink to deepen the shade. This worked much better, and after I attached the title to my page, I added dimensional glaze for extra shine.

Photo: Lorraine Powell, Victoria, British Columbia, Canada

I wish you the
beginnings of all your dreams
and many of the ends. - Mary Ann Radmacher

Perfection..... at two months old.
Jolene Katherine Powell - April 28th 2005

i make
perfect sense
to me sometimes.
unknown

Use a quote to create a smaller embellishment

This fun page embellishment would make a great addition to any carefree page. White cardstock was cut slightly smaller than an acrylic frame, and the two were stitched together with pink thread. Strips of verse were matted on blue and layered over the opening of the frame. Scraps of ribbon, wire and buttons add a splash of color while adhesive jewels add just the right amount of sparkle. I finished by adhering the frame to a pale lime cardstock mat with dimensional foam tape.

Create a chipboard monogram

Chipboard makes the perfect foundation to alter into funky page embellishments. Here I covered the chipboard base with an even application of adhesive and then with patterned paper. I trimmed it to size and sanded the edges. I then covered the monogram with a co-ordinating patterned paper and sanded and inked the edges. I tied patterned paper circles to clear buttons with blue wire and adhered them to the monogram. I added the remaining parts of verse and strips of rickrack to the base. I punched holes along the left side, set eyelets in the holes and added pretty ribbons and a metal chain through the holes. Lastly, I placed the monogram letter back into the opening using adhesive foam tape to give additional dimension.

Quote: Unknown

Use chipboard to create unique embellishments

This page embellishment is another great example of how versatile a chipboard base can be. After selecting several coordinating papers from my scrap box, I used an acrylic flourish stamp to stamp the image to the aqua paper with a medium-toned gray ink. This helps to fill and "grunge up" the background so it matches the other papers. Striped papers were added to the top and bottom of the chipboard base, and their seams were covered with velvet ribbon. After adding the verse, antique charms were used as photo anchors. Scalloped trim finishes off this rich look.

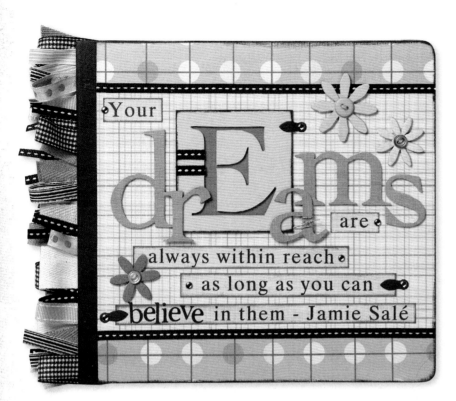

Adorn a mini album with a meaningful quote

Circle journals and mini books have become an addictive part of scrapbooking, and their embellished covers really set the tone of the album. With the abundance of quotes and sayings that can be found in books and on the Internet, you can be sure to find the right verse for just about any theme. The one I used here I knew would be perfect for a mini album for my daughter as she enters her teen years, and since most mini books can easily be taken apart and the covers removed, decorating it was a snap.

Use dye to coordinate colors

Dyes are a great way to customize items to better match other items used in your projects. On this border the cotton lace, jewelry tags and paper flowers were dyed with a blue scrapbook dye. Although it was a much better match to my papers than their original stark white, they were still a bit too "clean" looking for the distressed look of my papers. An additional swipe of a brown inkpad toned them down and now they are a perfect fit with all of my other elements. See sketch on page 101.

ALEX
TRUDY
& AYSHA

YOU WILL FIND AS YOU LOOK BACK
UPON YOUR **life** THAT THE
MOMENTS
WHEN YOU HAVE
TRULY LIVED ARE THE
{**moments**}
WHEN YOU HAVE
DONE THINGS IN THE
SPIRIT OF
love

ONE BEAUTIFUL SUMMER'S DAY THE KIDS AND

I SPENT A TREASURED DAY TOGETHER IN NANAIMO.

AUGUST 2001

— HENRY DRUMMOND

Use ribbon for a background

If you are anything like me, you have an abundance of ribbon…more ribbon than you are ever likely to use, and yet you can't help adding to your stash. So I like to dig into my ribbon box and find the perfect ones to create delicately textured backgrounds for my pages. After cutting a sheer patterned ribbon into strips and attaching them to cardstock with a vellum adhesive, I added a handcut cardstock heart which reinforces the page's "love" theme while providing a perfect solid foundation to build the verse on. Large funky sequin flowers and additional machine-stitching finish off this fun page.

A tiny bouquet of **FLOWERS**

Can fill a room with sunshine

A tiny act of **kindNEss**

Can fill a heart with joy

ALEX'S

MAY 2001

Add distressed focal letters

I have been blessed with having the sweetest and most loving son, as is apparent in this layout. He had been on a play date at a friend's house and came home carrying having a bunch of flowers that he proudly presented to me. To give emphasis to the word "gift" I used premade glossy chipboard letters that had a distressed appearance. The worn look blends nicely with the sanded papers, flowers and soft blues and greens.

Quote: Unknown

Tip from Trudy

Rickrack works great as a background accent to large focal words. It lends a fun, funky rhythm and is easy to adhere to cardstock or patterned paper.

"Live as if you were going to die tomorrow.

Learn as if you were going to

live

forever" - Gandhi

Use machine-stitching to accent

Machine-stitching is one of my favorite techniques to use on my scrapbooking and paper craft projects. It is simple to do, you don't need to be able to sew straight and it complements any style from hip and funky to rich and elegant. When in the last stages of making this border, I felt it was missing something. I knew I wanted to keep it relatively simple, but it still needed something more. Once I added the black stitching the whole look pulled together and became balanced and complete.

1 Quote, 3 Variations

I gave designers Karen Cobb and Sandra Ash this quote by Ralph Waldo Emerson and asked them to use a vintage color scheme. You can see the different ways we all chose to embellish the verse.

Use walnut ink to dye

I love the look you can achieve by hand-dyeing items in walnut ink. The problem is that I don't always want to wait while the items take the necessary time to dry. To avoid this, I generally dye larger quantities of tags, twill or muslin at one time so I always have some on hand and ready to use. Here, I sewed a large strip of patterned paper to multiple-dyed tags for the base of my border, and then added additional smaller strips of patterned papers and text. I stitched around each of the text boxes, painted a layer of walnut ink over cardstock letter stickers and applied a coat of dimensional glaze to create the perfect match to the other elements. Torn strips of hand-dyed muslin complete this vintage border.

Use a self-adhesive mask to create an image

Sandra took an interesting approach to the background treatment of her border. She applied a self-adhesive mask to the stripe patterned paper and inked on top of it with a brayer. Once the ink was dry, she removed the reusable mask and was left with the subtle image of a floral bouquet. Sandra then broke her verse into five different sections, which were printed onto patterned paper. Finally, she added her focal words to each section along with a touch of simple embellishments.

by Sandra

APPLY TEXTURE MAGIC TO LETTERS

1 Punch letter using a die-cut machine and font die. Using a temporary adhesive, place the negative image faceup on desired cardstock.

2 Mix Texture Magic with a small amount of gold craft paint. Evenly spread this mixture over letter image. Be sure that the negative space is completely filled with the mixture and scrape smooth.

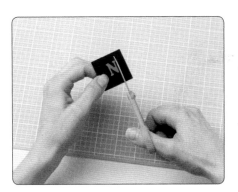

3 Carefully remove the negative image. Once mixture is completely dry, cut into a letter tile with a craft knife or scissors.

Combine a variety of word treatments

Karen's choice of photos was ideally suited for this quote as her page recounts the story of Billy Barker discovering gold deposits on the banks of Williams Creek resulting in the development of the historical town of Barkerville in central British Columbia. Karen cleverly combined different word treatments and textures (see step-by-step instructions) to make the verse the predominant embellishment on this great page.

by Karen

Embellish with lace and fabric

I have always loved using lace and fabrics on my scrapbook pages, and as soon as I saw these wide eyelet lace borders in the fabric store, I knew I had to buy some. On this page I used one strip of 6" (15 cm) deep lace and three strips of 3" (7.6 cm) deep lace. The 3" (7.6 cm) strips were dyed in walnut ink, but because I wanted three different shades, I first dyed one strip and hung it to dry. The second strip was dyed and allowed to partially dry, then rinsed under water. This gave me a lighter shade. The final piece of lace was dyed in the ink, set aside to dry and then dyed again, giving me the darkest shade. Once they were all dry, they were layered across the page and secured to the back with adhesive tape. The taupe silk flowers and measuring twill tape were also dyed with the walnut ink crystals.

Song lyrics: "Closing Time" written by Dan Wilson

Create a feminine border

Pink, black and white is one of my favorite color combinations, and this border makes a cute addition to any "girly" page. Sew strips of patterned papers to pink cardstock with black thread. Print the text on white cardstock by reformatting your text box so the fill color is pink and the font color is white (as shown on page 78). Trim the text into strips and attach to white shipping tags with brads. Die-cut flowers make cute tag toppers when combined with eyelets and ribbons, while colorful twill tape, mini page pebbles and additional die-cut flowers complete this funky border.

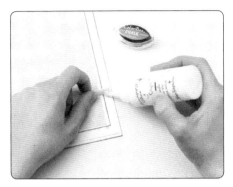

1 Start by making the basic foundation of the page; this will be the part that is behind the frame and can be up to ¼" (.6 cm) thick.

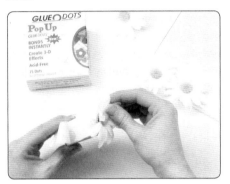

2 Add the flowers to the bottom of the frame using a strong adhesive. (Note: When adding anything to the front of your frame, make sure to always have your page behind the frame to make sure that you are lining up your elements correctly.)

3 Attach the photograph to a chipboard base to give it additional dimension and attach the photo to the outside of the frame. Add verse block (with focal words missing) to the actual page and replace the page behind the frame, again for correct placement of your remaining elements. Complete the verse by adding letter stickers for the focal word to the outside of the frame. Finish by adding rub-ons and sparkly jewels. Use decorative ribbons to hang.

Find inspiration in everyday life

You don't always have to turn to books or the Internet to find the perfect quote. I was sitting watching Oprah on TV while she was interviewing actor Orlando Bloom about his time in the South helping Hurricane Katrina victims when she said to him, "The future is so bright for you it burns my eyes." I was immediately taken by those words and wrote them down in the back of a quote book so I wouldn't forget them. When I sat down to make this scrapbook wall art (see step-by step instructions) for my friend's daughter, I thought this verse was perfect for a page about a child with great opportunities ahead of her.

Photo: Tara Tuck, Victoria, British Columbia, Canada

Repeat patterns for unity

When planning out your layouts, look for subtle shapes or patterns in your photographs and play up those elements with your page design. Trimming the focal photo into a circular shape emphasizes the circular hole in the playground equipment my daughter is looking through. Using metal-rimmed circular letters for my highlighted words further supports the design. After I completed my basic design, I realized that I didn't have the room I wanted for my journaling, so I created a pocket behind the top left corner of my large photo and tucked in my two journaling mats behind that. See sketch on page 101.

adore

love

All you need is to be you

Your true self shines with more beauty

than your eyes can see

Juan de Fuca Rec Center, Colwood, B.C. Summer 2004

AYshA

— Flavia

Pull

Aysha you're growing and changing so fast. One moment I look at you and you are still my little girl. But then the next moment, you are on the verge of being a teenager with all

Pull

of the issues that come along with it. If you don't remember half of what I have said over the years please remember this one thing . . . to always be yourself. You are a beautiful person inside & out. I love you!

Add verse to a circular element

I love the texture of the stone engraving that my son is standing next to and wanted to play up those textures with my choice of papers. Pieces of patterned papers were sewn to the foundation with black stitching. One of the papers had random circles, some of which I trimmed, stitched and layered to the page. The chipboard bookplate was originally pink and not quite what I had in mind, so I applied a layer of adhesive to the front, covered it with matching paper, trimmed and inked it. Then it worked perfectly for the page. Additional touches of zigzag stitching and distressed rub-on letters help to complete the look. See sketch on page 102.

BE

Alex

brave.
Even if you're not
pretend
to be.
No one can tell the
difference
— H. Jackson Brown

nOv '01

In nanaimo

Alex, you can accomplish anything you put your mind to as you are stronger than you realize. Just try hard, be brave, stay strong and always, always remember you are loved!

SAND AND EMBOSS LETTERS TO ADD DEFINITION

1 Using temporary adhesive, attach die-cut letters to a piece of cardstock.

2 Lay your paper on top of the die-cut letters and lightly sand over the letters to see your image. (This will only work with papers that have a white core.) Use an embossing stylus to run around the edges of the letters to give them added definition.

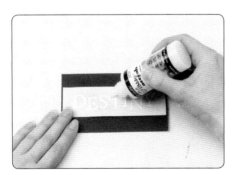

3 Finish by adding a layer of dimensional glaze over each letter. Set to one side and allow glaze to dry.

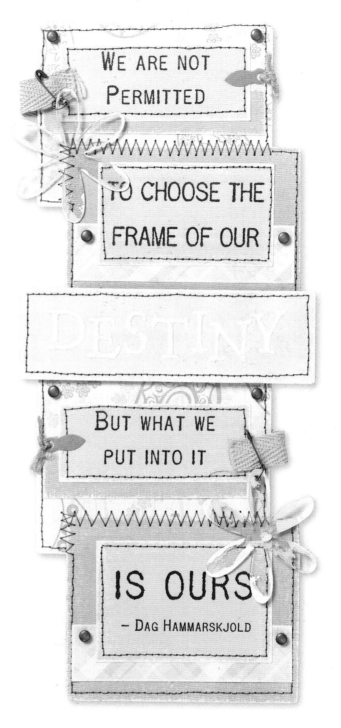

Overlap papers

I hate having to cut up full sheets of patterned papers and then be left with so many scraps, so I like to utilize my leftover pieces as much as I can. This was the case with this border, which was made completely from papers in my scrap box. Four 3 x 4" (7.6 cm x 10.2 cm) rectangles of coordinating papers were sanded and stitched together so that they overlapped. The focal word from the verse (see step-by-step instructions) was attached to the center of the verse with dimensional foam tape. Painted ghost flowers hanging from twill tape tabs add personality while antique scrapbook nails add just the right finishing touch. See sketch on page 102.

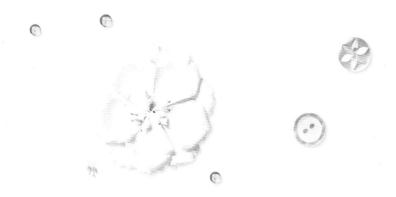

Keep it clean and simple

For this particular border, I decided to keep things simple. Horizontal strips of patterned papers not only add visual interest to the background but also give a sense of balance to the strong vertical lines of the larger text boxes and the border itself. Subtle touches of twine and gray mini page pebbles along with heavy inking add just enough pizazz to keep the border simple but not boring. See sketch on page 102.

Spread your wings *and prepare to fly,*

March 21, 1998

Kristine Petronella Tolsma

July 6th, 2004

for you have become a Butterfly

~Mariah Carey & Walter Afanasieff

Use embellishments to balance

Although tribute pages may be the hardest type of layouts to create, they can play the most important role in what makes your albums so meaningful to you and your family. Layers of lightly inked patterned papers were sewn with strips of lace and satin ribbons. Antique buttons help balance the visual weight of the page and create a base for the handcut word "butterfly" to rest on. Delicate flowers add some contrast, and butterfly charms help reinforce the theme of the verse while the single heart charm signifies that this special child will always be loved.

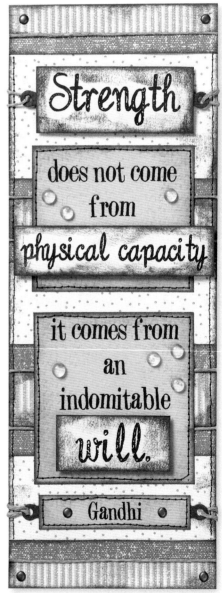

Strength

does not come from

physical capacity

it comes from an indomitable will.

• Gandhi •

ACCENT COVER WITH STAIN AND RUB-ONS

1 Lay the cover of the album flat on a sheet of wax paper. Using a foam brush, paint the cover with a layer of walnut ink. Immediately sprinkle coarse salt over the cover and allow to dry. (The cover must be wet with ink or the salt can't draw up the ink and you will not get the desired look. Spray the cover with additional walnut ink or water if needed.)

2 Once the cover has dried, brush off the salt crystals and paint the cover with a layer of gold glaze. Allow to dry thoroughly.

3 Apply the rub-on border along the side of the front of the cover.

Personalize a mini album

I love to personalize my mini albums and make them one-of-a-kind. What a great gift to make for someone (or even yourself!). The cover of this book was originally white, and I viewed it as a blank canvas just waiting to be decorated. After I stained the cover (see step-by-step instructions), I added an ornate rub-on border and rich satin trim. Layers of mica tiles frame the verse that was stamped on a walnut-inked tag and painted with the same gold glaze as the cover. Punch out die-cut typewriter letters and attach to the center of metal washers, then cover the letters with a layer of dimensional glaze. Once the glaze is dry, add the typewriter letters to the center of your verse.

Break verse into sections

As I was reading this verse in my head, I found that I was naturally breaking the verse into four sections with the focal word at the end of each section. I decided to go along with that idea for my design, and die-cut letters worked perfectly to highlight those focal words. The paper I chose to use for my sections of verse actually had flowers on it, not what I had in mind for this design. By trimming the paper into smaller sections and adding distress ink, I was able to give it a more masculine feel and the flowers just became more of a subtle background shape. Strips of ribbon adorned with ribbon buckles, index tabs and machine-stitching give the border just the right finishing touches.

Add unity by repeating circular elements

Even though she was working with a masculine color scheme, as a mother of three girls, Karen naturally put a more feminine twist to her border by adding sheer ribbon bows. This smaller-sized border, perfect for Karen's 8½ x 11" (21.6 cm x 27.9 cm) scrapbooks, has a unique border along the left side. Small circle punches play upon the dotted background paper and circular pieces of text. Karen also had a coordinating sheet of stickers that contained mats with pre-printed words. She liked the mats, but the words didn't work with those in the verse, so Karen printed portions of the poem onto matching papers and layered them onto the sticker mats.

by Karen

EXPERIMENT WITH TEXTURE PASTE AND BUBBLE WRAP

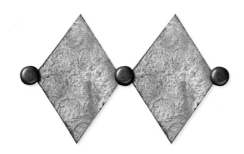

1 *Draw out a diamond pattern onto a piece of chipboard. On the reverse side, cover with a layer of green paint. Spread a thin layer of texture paste over the painted surface.*

2 *Press a piece of bubble wrap into the wet texture paste and remove. Allow the paste to dry. (Although Sandra used bubble wrap, this will work perfectly with many other textured surfaces or stamps.)*

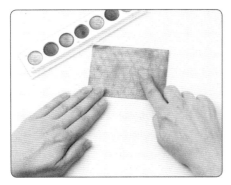

3 *Apply metallic rub-ons to the textured surface to highlight the pattern made by the bubble wrap. Trim into pieces following the pattern drawn on the reverse side.*

Create a harlequin design

Sandra used this quote on a touching layout for her son, Jake. Large rectangles of patterned papers were inked, layered and stitched to a cardstock foundation. Sections of the verse and journaling were printed and then framed with a border stamp and stitching to create unique mats for her words. Lastly, Sandra used texture paste and bubble wrap to create a harlequin design (see step-by-step instructions) that perfectly finishes off this classically styled page.

by Sandra

Sketches

I sketch out my designs when I am creating borders and pages embellished with quotes and poems because I want the text from the verse to take form as part of the project's overall design, rather than just as something in a matted text block. By creating a sketch first, I know how much space the verse will need, what size and how many photos I can include, if and where I will be including additional journaling and if the verse will also take place as part of the title. I also find the sketch to be an invaluable tool when turning to the computer to experiment with different fonts, point sizes and character spacing.

The following pages feature sketches from 20 pieces of art featured in this book. Study them to see how much easier the designs are when you break them down. So often the colors and patterns of the products we use can make it more difficult to see the actual blueprint of the design. Use these to help you re-create some of the original artwork, or combine different elements from several sketches to make up something new. Or use these purely as inspiration while you create your own one-of-a-kind designs.

Life

Page 21

Cherished Memories

Page 6

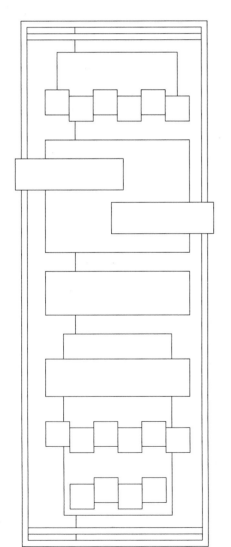

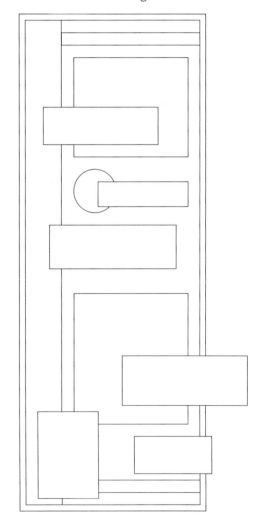

When I Look at My Child

Page 22

Generations

Page 29

I Love You

Page 36

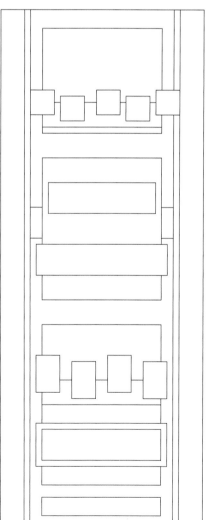

If Even a Day

Page 36

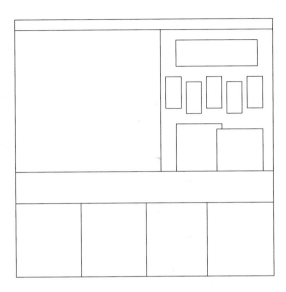

One Little Smile

Page 40

One Moment

Page 41

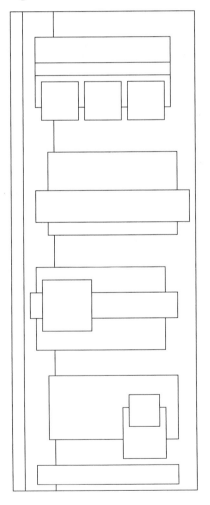

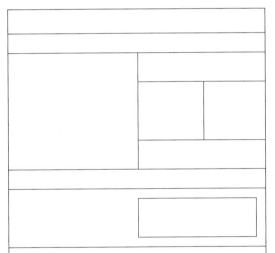

4 Feet

Page 55

Camp Thunderbird

Page 58

First Snow

Page 60

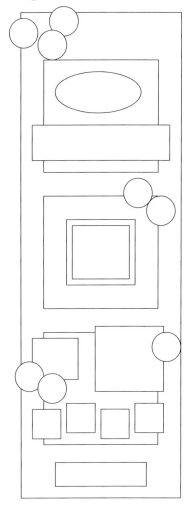

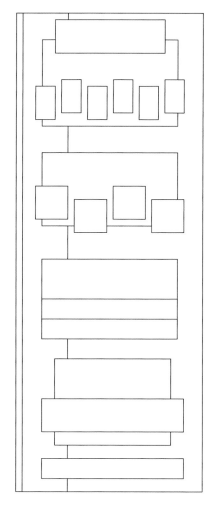

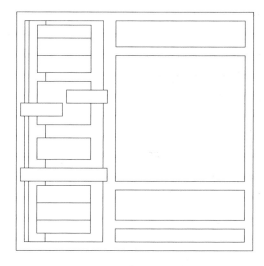

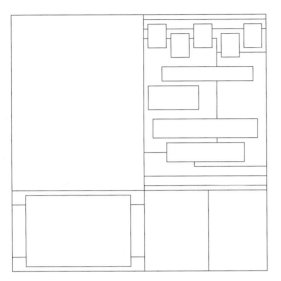

Flowers

Page 65

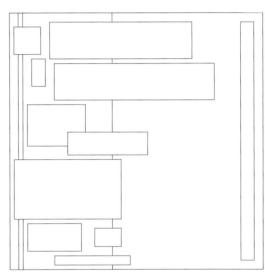

Watch the Leaves Turn

Page 71

The Heart of Autumn

Page 70

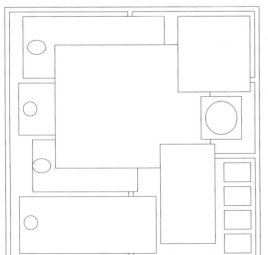

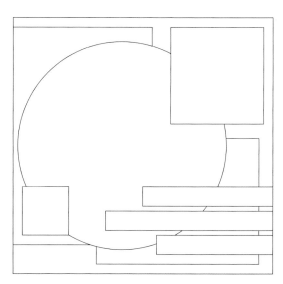

When the World Says Give Up

Page 77

There Will Come a Time

Page 82

Adore

Page 90

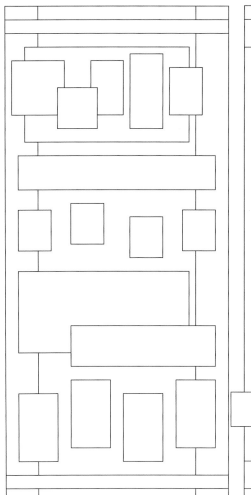

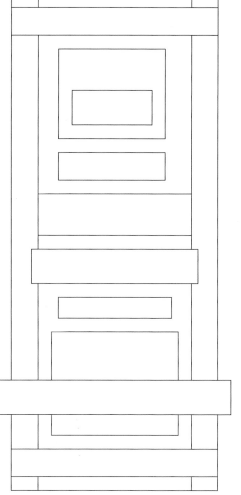

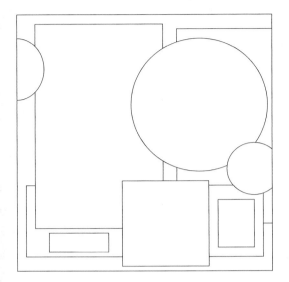

Be Brave
Page 90

Strength
Page 92

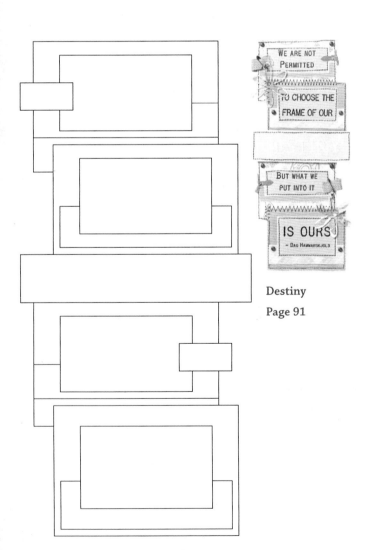

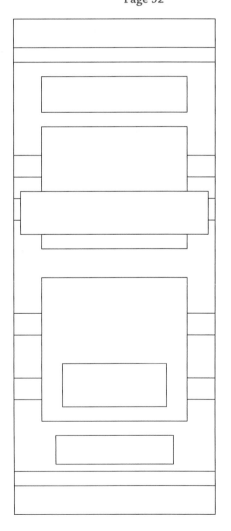

Destiny
Page 91

Supply lists

COVER

Patterned paper (Heidi Grace Designs); textured cardstock (Bazzill); cardstock (Doodlebug Design); die-cut tiles, letters (QuicKutz); chipboard ampersand, jewels (Heidi Swapp); brads, bookplate, dye (Making Memories); chalk ink (Clearsnap); computer fonts (2P's Gift, 2P's Evergreen, SP Purkage); cheesecloth; flower; ribbon; acrylic paint

LOVE DIVIDED ENDLESSLY/PAGE 1

Patterned papers (Collage Press); buttons (SEI); mini page pebbles (Memories in the Making); rub-on heart (Sandylion); love tiles (Me & My Big Ideas); computer fonts (2P's Tiger Tails, P22 Typewriter, Prissy Frat Boy); adhesives (Glue Dots International, Magic Scraps, Therm O Web); flowers; lace

CHERISHED MEMORIES/PAGE 6

Patterned paper, letter stickers (Creative Imaginations); wire, beads, eyelets (JewelCraft); heart charms (Quest Beads); insect charms (Nunn Design); metal letters (Global Solutions); computer fonts (www.twopeasinabucket.com); adhesives (Glue Dots International, Magic Scraps, Therm O Web); chalk (Craft-T); cardstock; jump rings; pen

A DREAM IS JUST A DREAM/PAGE 8

Patterned paper (Carolee's Creations, KI Memories); circle stamps, letter stamps (Carolee's Creations); textured cardstock, chipboard circles, monochromatic inks (Bazzill); chalk ink (Clearsnap); solvent ink (Tsukineko); ribbon, rickrack (May Arts); die-cut photo turns, letters, flowers (QuicKutz); mini page pebbles (Memories in the Making); circle punch (Creative Memories); computer font (2P's Pure Imagination); adhesives (Magic Scraps, Therm O Web); brads; charm; jump ring

FAMILY MEMORIES/PAGE 12

Patterned papers (Creative Imaginations); chipboard letters, hearts (Heidi Swapp); die-cut index tab (QuicKutz); distress ink, dimensional glaze (Ranger); photo turns (7 Gypsies); mini brads, textured cardstock (Bazzill); other brads (ScrapArts); date stamp (JustRite Stampers); adhesive foam squares (Therm O Web); computer font (Prissy Frat Boy); ribbon

BLOSSOM/PAGE 14

Patterned papers (Scenic Route Paper Co.); chipboard letters, acrylic paint, edge scraper (Making Memories); twill letters, letter stickers (Carolee's Creations); die-cut letters, embossing template (QuicKutz); chipboard shape, textured cardstock (Bazzill); paper flowers (Prima); distress ink (Ranger); ribbon (May Arts); metal heart (Q-T's); antique clip (Karen Foster Design); computer fonts (2P's Magic Forest, AL Worn Remington); adhesives (Magic Scraps, Therm O Web); antique brads; shipping tag

ONE SMILE/PAGE 14

Patterned paper (Melissa Frances); alphabet playing cards (Creative Imaginations); paper flowers (Serendipity Designworks); die-cut letters, photo turns, tag (QuicKutz); chipboard hearts (Heidi Swapp); chalk ink (Clearsnap); rub-on word (Sandylion); mini page pebbles (Memories in the Making); computer font (P22 Typewriter); adhesives (Magic Scraps, Therm O Web); cardstocks; ribbon; brads

GOD'S GIFT/PAGE 15

Patterned paper (My Mind's Eye); letter stamps (Ma Vinci's Reliquary, My Sentiments Exactly, River City Rubber Works); stamping ink, distress ink (Ranger); walnut ink (7 Gypsies); rub-on letters (Autumn Leaves); dimensional glaze (Ranger); square punch (Creative Memories); die-cut nameplate (QuicKutz); scrapbook nails (Chatterbox); computer font (P22 Typewriter); adhesives (Magic Scraps, Therm O Web); cardstock; lace; satin flowers

A LITTLE GIRL/PAGE 16

Patterned paper (My Mind's Eye); chipboard hearts (Heidi Swapp); distress ink (Ranger); letter stamps (PSX Design); date stamp (JustRite Stampers); computer fonts (Marcelle Script, Twylite Zone-Book); adhesives (Magic Scraps, Therm O Web); brads; lace

FAMILY/PAGE 17

Patterned paper, border stickers, flower and dragonfly stickers (Sandylion); die-cut letters (QuicKutz); letter stamps (Ma Vinci's Reliquary); jewels (Me & My Big Ideas); ribbon (May Arts); cheesecloth (Whimpole St.); acrylic paint (Making Memories); scrapbook nails (Chatterbox); textured cardstock (Bazzill); adhesives (Glue Dots International, Magic Scraps, Therm O Web)

JOY/PAGE 17

Patterned paper (K & Company); textured cardstock, chipboard circle, stamping ink (Bazzill); premade flowers (EK Success); beads (Me & My Big Ideas); die-cut re-enforcement (AccuCut); heart charm (Once Upon A Charm); computer font (Clarissa); adhesives (Glue Dots International, Magic Scraps); flower; lace; ribbon

BABY LIFE/PAGE 18

Patterned paper (Junkitz); chipboard letter (Li'l Davis Designs); textured cardstock (Bazzill); rub-on letters (Chatterbox, Making Memories); distress ink (Stewart Superior); fabric tab (Scrapworks); ribbons (American Crafts, May Arts); heart charm (Quest Beads); adhesives (Magic Scraps, Therm O Web); brads; jump ring; lace; safety pin

RAISING MY CHILDREN/PAGE 18

Patterned papers (7 Gypsies, Creative Imaginations); chipboard heart (Heidi Swapp); rickrack (Memories in the Making); extreme eyelet (Creative Imaginations); metal chain, brads (Making Memories); chalk ink (Clearsnap); die-cut re-enforcement (AccuCut); computer fonts (2P's Evergreen, 2P's Gift); adhesives (Magic Scraps, Therm O Web); cardstock

MEMORIES/PAGE 19

Patterned paper (KI Memories); textured cardstocks (Bazzill); die-cut flowers, photo turns, die-cut flowers (QuicKutz); distress ink (Stewart Superior); computer fonts (2P's Beef Broccoli, Wazoo Boxed Cap); adhesives (Magic Scraps, Therm O Web); brads; ribbon

HEROS & SONS/PAGE 20

Patterned paper (My Mind's Eye); textured cardstock (Bazzill); letter stamps (River City Rubber Works); distress ink (Ranger); solvent ink (Tsukineko); rub-on letters, rub-on flower (Autumn Leaves); twill heart (Carolee's Creations) die-cut tag (QuicKutz); ribbon (May Arts); buttons (Memories in the Making); art hooks (Li'l Davis Designs); epoxy word (Creative Imaginations); computer font (Weathered SF); linen thread (Hillcreek Designs); photo turns (Making Memories); adhesives (Magic Scraps, Therm O Web); brads

BOY/PAGE 21

6 x 6" album, blue and green papers, monogram sticker, heart charm (Heidi Grace Designs); metal letters (American Crafts); letter stamps (Carolee's Creations); die-cut tile, index tabs (QuicKutz), stamping ink, chipboard circle (Bazzill); mini page pebbles (Memories in the Making); rickrack (Doodlebug Design, Memories in the Making); ribbons (May Arts); circle punches (Creative Memories); solvent ink (Tsukineko); chalk ink (Clearsnap); adhesives (Magic Scraps, Therm O Web); cardstock

LIFE/PAGE 21

Patterned paper, letter and flower stickers, acrylic tags, hearts and blocks, rectangular brads (Heidi Grace Designs); textured cardstock, monochromatic inks (Bazzill); ribbon (May Arts); rickrack (Memories in the Making); die-cut photo turns (QuicKutz); rub-on letters (Autumn Leaves); computer font (Tiempo); adhesives (Magic Scraps, Therm O Web); eyelets

MY CHILD/PAGE 22

Patterned paper, die-cut frame, letter tiles, tag (Déjà Views); letter stamps (Gel-a-Tins); flowers, buttons, rickrack (Memories in the Making); distress ink, dimensional glaze (Ranger); stamping ink (Close To My Heart); ribbon (May Arts); computer fonts (2P's Bad Hair Day, 2P's Ragtag, Westwood LET); label maker (Dymo); embroidery floss (DMC); adhesives (Glue Dots International, Tombow); cardstock

WHEN I LOOK AT MY CHILD/PAGE 22

Patterned paper (Imagination Project); textured cardstock, monochromatic inks (Bazzill); rub-on letters, sticker squares, heart charm tags (Heidi Grace Designs); die-cut letters, mini tags (QuicKutz); ribbon (Scrapworks); jewels (Heidi Swapp); adhesives (Magic Scraps, Therm O Web, Xyron); brads; eyelets

CHILD/PAGE 23

Patterned paper (Imagination Project, Junkitz); rickrack, microscope slides, mini page pebbles (Memories in the Making); alcohol ink, blending solution, stamping ink (Ranger); letter stickers (American Crafts); rub-on letters (My Mind's Eye); paper flowers (Prima); embossing powder (PSX Design); double-sided tape (Provo Craft); cardstock; silk flowers; pen

ALWAYS REMEMBER/PAGE 24

Patterned paper (Daisy D's); cardstock (Bazzill, Making Memories); letter and square stamps (Gel-a-Tins); stamping ink (Rubber Stampede, Tsukineko); monogram rub-on, woven label (Me & My Big Ideas); button, chipboard circle (Bazzill); butterfly charm (K & Company); die-cut letters, tag (QuicKutz); letter stickers (Carolee's Creations); dimensional glaze (Ranger); paper flowers (Prima, Serendipity Designworks); ribbon (Offray); computer font (Tweedledee); adhesives (Glue Dots International, Magic Scraps, Therm O Web, Tombow); silk flowers; paper clip heart; fibers; ribbon; cotton lace; brads

CHILDREN'S HANDS/PAGE 25

Patterned papers (Autumn Leaves); distress ink (Ranger); chalk (Craf-T); ribbon (Textured Trios); foam stamp, acrylic paint (Making Memories); buttons, mini page pebbles, photo turns (Memories in the Making); paper flowers (Serendipity Designworks); adhesives (Magic Scraps, Therm O Web); brads; cardstock; computer fonts

CHILDREN'S HANDS (HEART)/PAGE 25

Patterned paper (Chatterbox); die-cut letters, stitching stamp, letter stamps (Carolee's Creations); chipboard hearts, photo anchors, brads (Making Memories); chipboard rectangle (Heidi Swapp); rub-on letters (Imagination Project); decorative edge scissors (Fiskars); distress ink, stamping ink (Ranger); wooden heart (Lara's Crafts); ribbon (May Arts); linen thread (Hillcreek Designs); computer font (Sandra's Print); silk flower; vintage buttons

A PARENT'S LOVE/PAGE 26

Patterned paper, cardstock sticker flowers, letters, tag, index tabs, rub-on flowers, clear letter stickers (Sandylion); clear nameplate, photo turn (QuicKutz); clear buttons (7 Gypsies); letter stamps (PSX Design); chalk ink (Clearsnap); stamping ink (Stewart Superior); ribbon (May Arts); adhesives (Magic Scraps, Therm O Web, Xyron); computer font (source unknown); brads; cardstock; lace

NO GIFT TO YOUR MOTHER/PAGE 27

Double-sided cardstocks, distressed flower rub-on, chocolate ribbon, blue frame (My Mind's Eye); acrylic paint, small chipboard letters, safety pin (Making Memories); large chipboard letters (Heidi Swapp); thick lace (Rusty Pickle); walnut ink (7 Gypsies); chipboard circle (Bazzill); ribbon snap (Melissa Frances); die-cut index tab (Sizzix); ribbon buckle (Memories in the Making); distress ink (Ranger); date stamp (JustRite Stampers); computer font (Selfish); adhesives (Glue Dots International, Magic Scraps, Therm O Web); cheesecloth (Whimpole St.); brads; charms; flowers; jump rings; lace

HEROS UNAWARE/PAGE 27

Patterned paper, tag, letter stickers (Basic Grey); chipboard letters (Li'l Davis Designs); chipboard stars (Heidi Swapp); acrylic paint, screw eyelets (Making Memories); date, letter stamps (JustRite Stampers); die-cut index tab (Sizzix); rub-on letters (Chatterbox); ribbon (Textured Trios); rickrack (Memories in the Making); distress ink (Stewart Superior); adhesives (Magic Scraps, Therm O Web); button

ANCESTORS/PAGE 28

Patterned paper (Junkitz); paper flowers (Prima); letter stamps (River City Rubber Works); epoxy stencil letters (Li'l Davis Designs); stamping ink (Tsukineko); distress ink (Ranger); walnut ink crystals (7 Gypsies); photo anchors (Making Memories); brads (Bazzill); beads (Me & My Big Ideas); computer fonts (JSL Ancient, P22 Corinthia); adhesives (Glue Dots International, Magic Scraps, Therm O Web); charms; doilies; lace; ribbon

BELONG TO THE PAST/PAGE 29

Patterned paper (Basic Grey); molding strip, acrylic paint, brads (Making Memories); letter stamps (Gel-a-Tins); distress ink, dimensional glaze (Ranger); walnut ink, rub-ons (7 Gypsies); chalk ink (Clearsnap); solvent ink (Tsukineko); die-cut tiles (QuicKutz); charms (Blue Moon Beads); computer font (CheltPress); adhesives (Glue Dots International, Magic Scraps, Therm O Web); flowers; lace

GENERATIONS/PAGE 29

Patterned paper, walnut ink crystals (7 Gypsies); letter stamps (EK Success, PSX Design, River City Rubber Works); foam dingbat stamps (Heidi Swapp); distress ink (Ranger); chalk ink (Clearsnap); stamping ink (Tsukineko); paper flowers (Prima); die-cut tags, tag topper, bookplate (QuicKutz); cardstock typewriter letters (Autumn Leaves); dimensional glaze (Ranger); mini page pebbles (Memories in the Making); linen thread (Hillcreek Designs); ribbon (May Arts, Me & My Big Ideas, Textured Trios); beads (Me & My Big Ideas); computer font (JSL Ancient); adhesives (Glue Dots International, Magic Scraps, Therm O Web); brads (Bazzill); metal washers; twill tape; shipping tags

WORKS OF ART/PAGE 30

Patterned paper (Basic Grey); cardstock (Colorbök); chipboard squares (Bazzill); chipboard letter (Making Memories) rub-on letters (Autumn Leaves, Making Memories, Me & My Big Ideas); date and letter stamps (JustRite Stampers); stamping ink (Clearsnap, Ranger, Tsukineko); ribbon (Me & My Big Ideas); fibers, silk ribbon (Yarn Collection); die-cut index tabs, tag, photo turns (QuicKutz); charm (Magenta); copper leafing pen (Krylon); adhesives (Glue Dots International, Magic Scraps, Therm O Web); computer fonts (American Scribe, Sandra Oh); brads; flowers; heart charm; jump ring

DELIGHTFUL GRANDCHILDREN/PAGE 31

Patterned paper (Scenic Route Paper Co.); textured cardstock, stamping ink (Bazzill); die-cut letters, mosaic tiles (QuicKutz); rickrack, mini page pebbles (Memories in the Making); paper flowers (Prima); chipboard rectangle (Heidi Swapp); ribbon (Creative Impressions); square brads (Making Memories); computer font (2P's Fancy Pants); adhesives (Magic Scraps, Therm O Web)

A GRANDPARENT'S LOVE/PAGE 32

Patterned paper, double-sided cardstock (Daisy D's); Roman and circle ("A") letter stamps (Gel-a-Tins); typewriter letter stamps (PSX Design); chipboard rectangles, brads (Bazzill); chipboard stars (Heidi Swapp); metal corners (Scrapworks); die-cut index tabs, photo turns (QuicKutz); rub-on letters (Autumn Leaves); cheesecloth (Wimpole St.); ribbon (Creative Impressions, May Arts, Offray); mini page pebbles (Memories in the Making); art hooks (Li'l Davis Designs); stamping ink (Tsukineko); chalk ink (Clearsnap); computer font (2P's Evergreen); adhesives (Glue Dots International, Magic Scraps); metal washer

TREASURE/PAGE 33

Patterned paper (7 Gypsies, Daisy D's); cardstocks (Bazzill, Colorbök); vintage letters (Autumn Leaves); letter stamps (River City Rubber Works); metal quote (Li'l Davis Designs); rub-on distressed tape measure (My Mind's Eye); paper flowers (Serendipity Designworks); distress ink (Ranger); chalk ink (Clearsnap); solvent ink (Tsukineko); walnut ink crystals (7 Gypsies); silk ribbon (Yarn Collection); ribbon (Creative Impressions, Textured Trios); postage stamp punch (EK Success); computer font (P22 Typewriter); adhesives (Glue Dots International, Magic Scraps, Therm O Web); photo anchors (Making Memories); brads; charms; clocks; jewelry findings; lace; vintage postage stamps

ANGEL'S HANDS/PAGE 34

Patterned paper (Carolee's Creations); chipboard letters (Heidi Swapp); rub-on letters (Autumn Leaves, Scrapworks); die-cut index tab, photo turns (QuicKutz); distress ink, dimensional glaze (Ranger); chipboard shapes, brads (Bazzill); acrylic paint (Making Memories); date stamp (JustRite Stampers); silk flower

I LOVE YOU/PAGE 36

Patterned paper, cardstock stickers, rub-on stitching, letter stickers (Sandylion); metallic ribbon (Yarn Collection); ribbon (May Arts); paper flowers (Prima); chalk ink (Clearsnap); jewels (Me & My Big Ideas); photo turns, mini brads (Making Memories); rub-on letters (Autumn Leaves); adhesives (Glue Dots International, Magic Scraps, Therm O Web); cardstock (Bazzill); computer font (Calson Antique); copper leafing pen (Krylon); lace

IF EVEN A DAY/PAGE 36

Patterned paper (Autumn Leaves); ribbon (Me & My Big Ideas, Sheer Creations); skeleton leaves, jump rings (Scrappin' Extras); charms (Blue Moon Beads); stamping ink (Bazzill, Stewart Superior); chalk (Craf-T); wire (Artistic Wire); adhesives (Glue Dots International, Magic Scraps, Therm O Web); stamps, mini brads (Making Memories); computer font (source unknown); lace; beads; cardstock

LOVE DOESN'T MAKE THE WORLD GO ROUND/PAGE 37

Textured cardstock (Keeping Memories Alive); ribbon (Creative Impressions, Making Memories, May Arts, Me & My Big Ideas, Textured Trios); walnut ink, flashcard, index tab, photo turns, rub-ons (7 Gypsies); twill labels, paper clip (Carolee's Creations); letter stamps (Gel-a-Tins, JustRite Stampers, PSX Design); date stamp (JustRite Stampers); distress ink (Ranger); solvent ink (Tsukineko); embellished backgrounds (Li'l Davis Designs); buttons (Jesse James); flowers (Serendipity Designworks); die-cut tags, tag toppers (QuicKutz); stick pin (Making Memories); adhesives (Glue Dots International, Magic Scraps, Therm O Web); silk flowers; brads

YOU HAD ME AT HELLO/PAGE 38

Album (Heidi Swapp); patterned cardstock (My Mind's Eye); die-cut flourishes, tags, index tab (QuicKutz); chipboard letters (Heidi Swapp, Making Memories); acrylic paint, metal chain, vellum tag, epoxy letter stickers, dye, safety pin, brads (Making Memories); wooden letters (Li'l Davis Designs); ribbon (Creative Impressions, May Arts); rickrack (Memories in the Making); fabric (Wimpole Street); charms (Blue Moon Beads, Quest Beads); zipper pull (All My Memories); stamps (PSX Design); stamping ink (Bazzill, Clearsnap); rub-on word (Sandylion); rub-on letters (Autumn Leaves); circle punch (EK Success); adhesives (Glue Dots International, Krylon, Magic Scraps); twill letters (Carolee's Creations); lace; flower; washers

LOVE IS BUT THE DISCOVERY/PAGE 39

Patterned paper (Me & My Big Ideas); rub-on letters (Autumn Leaves, My Mind's Eye); rub-on stitching, walnut ink, photo turns, handles (7 Gypsies); ribbon (May Arts); chipboard squares (Bazzill); die-cut flourishes (QuicKutz); distress ink (Ranger); chalk ink (Clearsnap); antique frame, epoxy word (Li'l Davis Designs); brads (Making Memories); computer font (Dominican Italic); cheesecloth (Wimpole Street); linen thread (Hillcreek Designs); lace; charms; flowers

TO LOVE AND BE LOVED/PAGE 39

Patterned paper (7 Gypsies, Carolee's Creations); letter stickers (Autumn Leaves); chipboard tiles, textured cardstock (Bazzill); acrylic paint, brads (Making Memories); photo turns, walnut ink (7 Gypsies); art hooks (Li'l Davis Designs); distress ink, dimensional glaze (Ranger); solvent ink (Tsukineko); mini page pebbles (Memories in the Making); letter stamps (EK Success); ribbon (Textured Trios); silk ribbon (Yarn Collection); adhesive (Magic Scraps); buttons; lace

ONE LITTLE SMILE/PAGE 40

Patterned papers (Chatterbox); die-cut flowers, photo turns (QuicKutz); rickrack, mini page pebbles (Memories in the Making); rubber letters (Scrapworks); letter stamps (Carolee's Creations); rub-on letters (Autumn Leaves); fabric tag (Creative Imaginations); solvent ink (Tsukineko); monochromatic ink, textured cardstock (Bazzill); chalk ink (Clearsnap); brads (ScrapArts); die-cut tag (AccuCut); computer fonts (Steelfish Outline, Times New Roman); adhesives (Glue Dots International, Magic Scraps, Therm O Web); ribbon; flower; eyelets; staples

THE BEST AND MOST BEAUTIFUL/PAGE 40

Patterned paper (Carolee's Creations); die-cut letters and tag (QuicKutz); chipboard flower, vellum tag, photo turns, safety pin (Making Memories); stamping ink (Clearsnap); ribbon (American Crafts, Textured Trios); mini page pebbles (Memories in the Making); rub-on letters (Sandylion); dimensional glaze (Ranger); round brads (Bazzill); rectangular brads (Heidi Grace Designs); computer font (Prissy Frat Boy); adhesives (Magic Scraps, Therm O Web); cardstock

STAR SMILE/PAGE 41

Patterned paper (My Mind's Eye); metal letters (American Crafts); die-cut nameplate, tag toppers, photo turns (QuicKutz); chipboard stars (Heidi Swapp); lace, metal chain (Making Memories); rub-on letters (Chatterbox); rub-on phrase (Me & My Big Ideas); chalk ink (Clearsnap); dimensional glaze (Ranger); brads (Bazzill); computer font (Distressed Typewriter); adhesive (Magic Scraps); charm; jump ring

ONE MOMENT/PAGE 41

Patterned papers, rub-on shapes (Autumn Leaves); textured cardstock, monochromatic ink, brads (Bazzill); rub-on letters, fabric tab (Scrapworks); die-cut index tab, tag (QuicKutz); chipboard heart (Heidi Swapp); letter stamps (Hero Arts); adhesives (Magic Scraps, Therm O Web); safety pin (Making Memories)

ONLY LOVE CAN BE DIVIDED/PAGE 42

Patterned papers (KI Memories, My Mind's Eye); brads (Creative Impressions, Making Memories); letter stamps (Carolee's Creations); stamping ink (Ranger); decorative scissors (Fiskars); chalk (Craf-T); computer font (Passions Conflict); cardstock; cheesecloth; thread; vintage buttons

ONLY LOVE/PAGE 42

Patterned papers (Autumn Leaves, Provo Craft); flowers, metal letters, label holder (Making Memories); letter stickers (Collage Press); monochromatic ink, brads (Bazzill); buttons (Chatterbox, Jesse James); die-cut word (Sizzix); die-cut photo turns (QuicKutz); photo corners (Heidi Swapp); dimensional glaze (Ranger); paint (Plaid); ribbon (May Arts); embroidery floss (DMC); computer font (Jot); adhesives (Magic Scraps, Therm O Web, Tombow); cardstock; ribbon

LOVE DIVIDED ENDLESSLY/PAGE 43

Patterned papers (Collage Press); buttons (SEI); mini page pebbles (Memories in the Making); rub-on heart (Sandylion); love tiles (Me & My Big Ideas); computer fonts (2P's Tiger Tails, P22 Typewriter, Prissy Frat Boy); adhesives (Glue Dots International, Magic Scraps, Therm O Web); flowers; lace; transparency

A REAL FRIEND/PAGE 44

Patterned papers, acrylic letters (KI Memories); double-sided cardstock (Doodlebug Design); ribbon (May Arts, Textured Trios); epoxy stickers (Me & My Big Ideas); die-cut letters, flowers, index tab, photo turns (QuicKutz); brads (Bazzill, Creative Impressions); rub-on letters (Scrapworks); chalk ink (Clearsnap); adhesives (Glue Dots International, Magic Scraps, Therm O Web); computer fonts (Auburn, Chewy Stewy, Doodolonomy Fred)

GOOD FRIENDS/PAGE 44

Patterned paper (Scrapbook Wizard); chipboard monogram (Heidi Swapp); chipboard letters, safety pins, brads, photo turns (Making Memories); braided lace (Me & My Big Ideas); index tab, walnut ink (7 Gypsies); photo anchor (Scrappin' Extras); letter stamps (PSX Design, River City Rubber Works); rub-on phrase (Sandylion); distress ink (Ranger); chalk ink (Clearsnap); solvent ink (Tsukineko); computer font (Weathered SF); adhesives (Glue Dots International, Magic Scraps, Xyron); cardstock; lace; ribbon; shipping tags; eyelets; flowers

YOU MEET PEOPLE YOU FORGET/PAGE 45

Patterned paper, double-sided cardstock (Keeping Memories Alive); letter stickers (American Crafts); ribbons (American Crafts, May Arts); rickrack (Doodlebug Design); flowers (Heidi Swapp); mini page pebbles (Memories in the Making); die-cut index tab (QuicKutz); chalk ink (Clearsnap); acrylic paint, edge scraper (Making Memories); letter stamps (PSX Design); brads (Bazzill); date stamp (JustRite Stampers); cheesecloth (Wimpole Street); adhesives (Magic Scraps); staples

A JOURNEY/PAGE 45

Patterned papers (Chatterbox, EK Success); chipboard circle (Bazzill); die-cut letters, index tab, photo turn (QuicKutz); rub-on letters (Me & My Big Ideas); paper flowers (Prima); rickrack (Memories in the Making); date stamp (JustRite Stampers); chalk ink (Clearsnap); computer font (Arial); adhesives (Magic Scraps, Therm O Web); buttons; lace

TRUE FRIENDSHIP/PAGE 46

Patterned paper (Scrapworks); letter stamps (Gel-a-Tins); textured cardstock, chipboard rectangle, brads (Bazzill); art hooks (Li'l Davis Designs); paper flowers (Prima); ribbon (May Arts); chalk ink (Clearsnap); solvent ink (Tsukineko); photo turns (Making Memories); dimensional glaze (Ranger); wire hearts (Q-T's); adhesives (Glue Dots International, Therm O Web)

FRIENDS ARE ANGELS/PAGE 46

Patterned paper (Fiber Scraps); textured cardstock, monochromatic ink (Bazzill); die-cut tags, embossing template (QuicKutz); flowers (Prima, Serendipity Designworks); letter stamps (EK Success); ribbon (May Arts); charms (Nunn Design); chalk ink (Clearsnap); photo turns, brads (Making Memories); computer fonts (Shalimar Swash); adhesives (Magic Scraps, Therm O Web); lace

FRIENDS WILL LEAVE FOOTPRINTS/PAGE 47

Patterned paper (Scenic Route Paper Co.); fabric letters (Scrapworks); chipboard hearts (Heidi Swapp, Making Memories); die-cut tags (QuicKutz); heart paper clip (Carolee's Creations); ribbon (May Arts); linen thread (Hillcreek Designs); distress ink (Ranger); chalk ink (Clearsnap); computer font (GF Halda); brads, safety pin (Making Memories); burlap

MY FRIENDS/PAGE 48

Album, cardstock, brads (Bazzill); stencil, chipboard letters, jewels (Heidi Swapp); dye, safety pin (Making Memories); chalk ink (Clearsnap); rickrack (Doodlebug Design, Memories in the Making); ribbon (American Crafts, Carolee's Creations, May Arts, Offray); twill tape (Creative Impressions); die-cut photo turns (QuicKutz); adhesives (Magic Scraps); computer font (CB Wednesday)

A FRIEND IS.../PAGE 49

Patterned paper (Imagination Project); textured cardstock (Bazzill); die-cut letters, photo turns (QuicKutz); distress ink (Ranger); walnut ink (7 Gypsies); chalk ink (Clearsnap); ribbon (Textured Trios); brads (Making Memories); computer font (Edifice); adhesives (Magic Scraps, Xyron); lace

DOGS/PAGE 50

Patterned paper (Paper Adventures); letter tiles (Li'l Davis Designs); chipboard tiles (Bazzill); letter stamps (PSX Design, River City Rubber Works); walnut ink (7 Gypsies); distress ink, dimensional glaze (Ranger); solvent ink (Tsukineko); chalk ink (Clearsnap); buttons (Jesse James); brads (Creative Impressions); adhesives (Magic Scraps); burlap; metal-rimmed tag; twill tape; metal charm

A DOG WAGS ITS TAIL/PAGE 51

Patterned paper (Chatterbox); chipboard rectangle, brads (Bazzill); metal letters, acrylic paint (Making Memories); buckle (www.maudeandmillie.com); computer font (Garamond); ribbon (Textured Trios); charm; staple

PETS ARE MIRACLES/PAGE 51

Patterned papers (Sandylion); rub-ons (Scrapworks); die-cut letters (QuicKutz); ribbon (American Crafts); paw charm (Go West Studios); distress ink (Ranger); walnut ink (7 Gypsies); acrylic paint, brads, jump ring (Making Memories); circle cutter (Provo Craft); adhesives (Glue Dots International, Magic Scraps, Xyron); lace

NEVER HOLD A DUSTBUSTER/PAGE 52

Patterned paper, twill tape, twill letters (Carolee's Creations); die-cut letters, photo turns (QuicKutz); acrylic mouse charm (Go West Studios); distress ink (Ranger); chalk ink (Clearsnap); acrylic paint, brads (Making Memories); computer font (Wiffles); adhesives (Glue Dots International, Magic Scraps)

CATS/PAGE 53

Patterned papers (Keeping Memories Alive); letter stickers (American Crafts, Chatterbox); acrylic tiles (Heidi Grace Designs); ribbon (Me & My Big Ideas, Textured Trios); photo turns (7 Gypsies); distress ink (Ranger); chalk ink (Clearsnap); brads (Making Memories); computer font (Ariel); adhesives (Glue Dots International, Magic Scraps, Therm O Web); cardstock

COMPANIONS/PAGE 54

Patterned papers (Autumn Leaves); textured cardstock, brads, monochromatic ink (Bazzill); acrylic flowers (KI Memories); die-cut tags, photo turns, tag topper die cuts (QuicKutz); rub-on letters (Making Memories); flower stamps (Gel-a-Tins); stamping ink (Stewart Superior); circle cutter (Provo Craft); computer fonts (2P's Chestnuts, 2P's Renaissance, 2P's Ring Ding, Tiempo); adhesives (Magic Scraps, Therm O Web); ribbon; transparency

OUR PERFECT COMPANIONS/PAGE 55

Patterned paper (Imagination Project); paper flowers (Prima); metal-rimmed tag, silver brads, eyelets, ribbon (Making Memories); brads, chipboard tile (Bazzill); wire (Artistic Wire); acrylic numeral (KI Memories); buttons (Jesse James); die-cut photo turns (QuicKutz); circle punches, lettering template (EK Success); letter stamps (All Night Media); stamping ink (Clearsnap, Close To My Heart); rub-on letters (Me & My Big Ideas); computer font (Doggie Bag Script); adhesives (Magic Scraps, Tombow, Therm O Web); cardstock; twill tape

4 FEET/PAGE 55

Patterned papers (Autumn Leaves); frames, tags, label, paw print rub-ons, stitching rubber stamp (Carolee's Creations); "four" sticker (Bo-Bunny Press); "perfect" sticker (K & Company); ribbon (May Arts); mini page pebbles (Memories in the Making); flowers (Prima, Serendipity Designworks); bookplate (Scrappin' Extras); stamping ink (Ranger); brads, photo turns (Making Memories); dimensional foam squares (Therm O Web); pen; buttons; wooden letter tiles

EACH DAY IS LIKE A SNOWFLAKE/PAGE 56

Patterned papers, cardstock stickers (Carolee's Creations); die-cut letters, photo turns (QuicKutz); dimensional glaze (Ranger); chalk ink (Clearsnap); adhesives (Xyron); dimensional foam squares (Therm O Web); computer font (Moonbeam Regular); mini brads; cardstock

CAMP THUNDERBIRD/PAGE 58

Patterned paper (Basic Grey); die-cut letters (QuicKutz); letter stamps (EK Success); ribbon, twill tape (Creative Impressions); buttons, photo turns (Memories in the Making); metal heart (Q-T's); chalk (Craf-T); distress ink (Ranger); walnut ink crystals (7 Gypsies); brads (ScrapArts); computer fonts (2P's Rickety, Crud Regular); adhesives (Glue Dots International, Therm O Web); twine; burlap; cardstock; jewelry tags

THE SUN/PAGE 59

Patterned papers (My Mind's Eye); die-cut letters, photo turns (QuicKutz); page pebbles, rickrack (Memories In The Making); paper flowers (Prima); dimensional glaze (Ranger); brads (Bazzill); adhesives (Glue Dots International, Magic Scraps, Xyron)

BEAUTIFUL WORLD/PAGE 59

Patterned papers (Creative Imaginations); ribbon (American Crafts); monochromatic ink pads, brads, textured cardstock (Bazzill); die-cut flourishes, index tab (QuicKutz); buttons (Memories In The Making); rub-on flower (7 Gypsies); photo turns (Making Memories); computer fonts (Dream Orphans, Rataczak Cond Plain); adhesives (Glue Dots International, Magic Scraps, Therm O Web)

FIRST SNOW/PAGE 60

Charm (Blue Moon Beads); dimensional glaze (Duncan); snowflake punches (Emagination Crafts); die-cut photo turns (QuicKutz); computer fonts (2P's Block Party, 2P's Glitter Girl, 2P's Winter Essential); adhesives (Glue Dots International, Magic Scraps, Therm O Web); ribbon; rickrack; beads; brads; eyelets; pen

SNOWFLAKES/PAGE 60

Patterned papers, rub-on letters (Autumn Leaves); chipboard letters (Pressed Petals); acrylic snowflakes, clear jewels (Heidi Swapp); blue jewels (JewelCraft); dimensional glaze (Ranger); photo turns (7 Gypsies); date stamp (JustRite Stampers); die-cut tag topper (QuicKutz); brads, textured cardstock (Bazzill); computer font (Rapid Normal); adhesives (Glue Dots International, Magic Scraps); stamping ink (Ranger); lace; safety pin; staple

CHRISTMAS TREE/PAGE 61

Patterned paper (Reminisce); die-cut letters, tag toppers (QuicKutz); distress ink (Ranger); chalk ink (Clearsnap); date stamp (JustRite Stampers); rickrack (Memories In The Making); mini brads, staples (Making Memories); linen thread (Hillcreek Designs); computer fonts (P22 Typewriter, Tiempo); adhesives (Magic Scraps, Xyron); cardstock; snowflake charms

CHRISTMAS WAVES A MAGIC WAND/PAGE 61

Flower punch (EK Success); computer font (Licorice, McBooHmk); adhesives (Glue Dots International, Magic Scraps, Therm O Web); beads; cardstock; ribbon; pen

SONG OF THE SEA/PAGE 62

Patterned paper (Carolee's Creations); letter stamps (FontWerks); jute mesh (Scrappin' Extras); mini page pebbles (Memories in the Making); distress ink (Ranger); computer font (Steelfish); adhesives (EK Success, Magic Scraps); twine; acrylic paint; cardstock; sand dollar charms

THE SEA/PAGE 62

Fish netting (U.S. Shell); letter stamps (Ma Vinci's Reliquary); walnut ink (7 Gypsies, Fiber Scraps); eyelets, safety pins, jump rings, photo turns (Making Memories); shells, liquid adhesive (Magic Scraps); die-cut tag (QuicKutz); linen thread (Hillcreek Designs); brads (Bazzill); computer font (P22 Typewriter); twine; cardstock; charms; acrylic paint; twine; muslin

THE SHORE/PAGE 63

Patterned paper, epoxy stickers (Me & My Big Ideas); rub-on letters (Me & My Big Ideas, My Mind's Eye); letter stickers (Wordsworth); mini page pebbles (Memories in the Making); alphabet ribbon charms, chipboard letters, heart, paper yarn, eyelets (Making Memories); sand (Activa Products); metal letters (American Crafts); buttons (Chatterbox, Making Memories); ribbon (Michaels, Offray); chipboard rectangle (Bazzill); punches (Creative Memories, EK Success); walnut ink (7 Gypsies); twill letters, letter brads (Carolee's Creations); safety pin, label holder (Scrappin' Extras); computer font (Rockwell); adhesive sheet (Provo Craft); adhesives (Glue Dots International, Tombow); cardstock; flower; slide mount; charms; cheesecloth; embroidery floss; acrylic paint; stamping ink; sand

A GARDEN/PAGE 64

Fabric strips (Homemade Memories); die-cut letters (QuicKutz); paper flowers (Serendipity Designworks); ribbon (May Arts, Textured Trios); clear photo turns (Junkitz); chalk ink (Clearsnap); corner rounder (McGill); charm (Quest Beads); brads, eyelets, safety pins (Making Memories); computer font (Times New Roman); adhesives (Glue Dots International, Magic Scraps, Therm O Web, Xyron); cardstock; chipboard; silk flowers; staples

EACH FLOWER/PAGE 64

Patterned paper (Chatterbox); paper flowers (Prima, Serendipity Designworks); mini page pebbles (Memories In The Making); computer fonts (2P's Flea Market, 2P's Unforgettable); adhesives (Magic Scraps, Therm O Web); cardstock; lace; ribbon; black pen

FLOWERS/PAGE 65

Patterned papers (Autumn Leaves); die-cut letters, flowers, index tab, tag topper, photo turns (QuicKutz); ribbon (American Crafts, May Arts); chalk ink (Clearsnap); computer fonts (Inkster, Wazoo); adhesives (Glue Dots International, Magic Scraps, Therm O Web); brads; cardstock; eyelets

ART OF GOD/PAGE 66

Patterned papers (Paper Adventures); die-cut letters (QuicKutz); flowers (EK Success); jewels (Heidi Swapp); die-cut tag re-enforcement (AccuCut); adhesives (Therm O Web); computer font (Garden Party); cardstock; eyelets; lace

SPRING/PAGE 67

Patterned papers, rivets (Chatterbox); die-cut letters (QuicKutz); paper flowers (Prima); mini page pebbles (Memories In The Making); chalk ink (Clearsnap); adhesives (Magic Scraps, Therm O Web, Xyron); computer font (Times New Roman); cardstock; lace; ribbon

LAUGH IN FLOWERS/PAGE 67

Acrylic frame, square brads (Heidi Grace Designs); die-cut letters (QuicKutz); textured cardstock (Bazzill); adhesives (Glue Dots International, Xyron); flower; twill tape

A PERFECT SUMMER/PAGE 68

Patterned papers (KI Memories); paper flowers (Prima, Serendipity Designworks); die-cut photo turns (QuicKutz); adhesives (Magic Scraps, Therm O Web); computer fonts (2P's A Little Loopy, 2P's Barefoot Professor, Wazoo Boxed Caps); beads; brads; cardstock; ribbon

A PICNIC/PAGE 68

Patterned paper, letter stamp (Carolee's Creations); ribbon (American Crafts, May Arts); acrylic flowers, chipboard heart, jewels (Heidi Swapp); chipboard flowers, safety pin (Making Memories); die-cut index tab (QuicKutz); chalk ink (Clearsnap); textured cardstock (National Cardstock); adhesives (Glue Dots International, Xyron); computer fonts (2P's Barefoot Professor, 2P's Chicken Shack, SP Purkage); staples; acrylic paint

LONG LIVE THE SUN/PAGE 69

Patterned papers (Basic Grey); acrylic monogram letter (Go West Studios); chipboard letters (Heidi Swapp, Making Memories); acrylic circle, photo turns (Junkitz); letter stickers (Chatterbox); jewels (Me & My Big Ideas); dimensional glaze (Ranger); chalk ink (Clearsnap); adhesives (Glue Dots International, Magic Scraps, Therm O Web, Xyron); cardstock; flowers; metallic leafing

THE HEART OF AUTUMN/PAGE 70

Patterned papers (Scenic Route Paper Co.); die-cut letters, tag, tag topper, index tab (QuicKutz); rub-on, metal index tab, photo turns (7 Gypsies); distress ink (Ranger); chalk ink (Clearsnap); brads, eyelets, jump rings (Making Memories); adhesives (Glue Dots International, Therm O Web); computer font (Prissy Frat Boy); cardstock; charm; twine

THE FOUR SEASONS/PAGE 70

Patterned papers, die-cut tags and leaves, ribbon (Scrapworks); die-cut letters, ampersand, photo turns (QuicKutz); die-cut tag re-enforcements (AccuCut); ribbon (American Crafts); distress ink (Ranger); eyelets, brads (Making Memories); adhesives (Glue Dots International, Magic Scraps, Therm O Web); computer font (Limehouse Script); textured cardstock (National Cardstock)

AUTUMN FLOWER/PAGE 71

Patterned papers, rubber letters, rub-on letters (Scrapworks); paper leaves (Prima); die-cut tag, tag toppers (QuicKutz); brads, eyelets (Making Memories); distress ink (Ranger); adhesives (Magic Scraps, Therm O Web); cardstock; acrylic paint; twine

WATCH THE LEAVES TURN/PAGE 71

Patterned papers (Daisy D's); rub-on images (Heidi Swapp); rub-on letters (Li'l Davis Designs, My Mind's Eye); letter stamps (Gel-a-Tins, PSX Design); date stamp, stick pins, brads, eyelets (Making Memories); square book plate, stitched leather strip, chipboard letter tiles (Li'l Davis Designs); walnut ink, photo turns, quote tag (7 Gypsies); vintage postal stamp letters (Autumn Leaves); fabric strips (Homemade Memories); distress ink (Ranger); chalk ink (Clearsnap); solvent ink (Tsukineko); heart (Provo Craft); rectangle bookplate (Memories in the Making)

DELIGHT IN THE BEAUTY/PAGE 72

Patterned paper (Paper Heart Studio); letter stickers (American Crafts, K & Company, Sandylion); rub-on distress elements (My Mind's Eye); metal frame, brads (Making Memories); spiral clip (Creative Impressions); ribbons (Michaels, Scraptivity Scrapbooking); die-cut name plate (QuicKutz); computer font (CB Brush Strokes, CB Wednesday, CBX Watson, Tilez); corner rounder (EK Success); adhesive (Tombow); flower; charm; cardstock; stamping ink

DELIGHT!/PAGE 72

Patterned paper (KI Memories); die-cut letters (QuicKutz); textured cardstock (Bazzill); ribbon (American Crafts); paper flowers (Serendipity Design Works); adhesives (Magic Scraps, Ross, Therm O Web, Xyron); computer font (Prissy Frat Boy); chipboard; staples; transparency

BEAUTY THAT SURROUNDS YOU/PAGE 73

Patterned papers (Chatterbox, My Mind's Eye); rickrack (May Arts); oven-bake clay (Polyform Products); rub-on letters, chipboard (Heidi Swapp); buttons (Memories in the Making); rubber stamp (FontWerks); photo turns (Making Memories); brads (Bazzill); stamping ink (Clearsnap, Versamark); flowers

YOU/PAGE 74

Textured cardstock, monochromatic ink (Bazzill); chipboard letters (Pressed Petals); acrylic circles (Junkitz); alcohol inks, blending solution, dimensional glaze (Ranger); die-cut index tab (QuicKutz); rub-on letters (Autumn Leaves); date stamp (JustRite Stampers); adhesive (Magic Scraps); computer font (Tiempo); ribbon; staples

THE WORLD IS LIKE A BOOK/PAGE 76

Letter stickers (American Crafts, Me & My Big Ideas); rub-on letters (Autumn Leaves); corner rounder (McGill); foam squares (Therm O Web); textured cardstock (National Cardstock); pen

WHEN THE WORLD SAYS/PAGE 77

Patterned papers (Sandylion); textured cardstock (Bazzill); die-cut photo turns, letters (QuicKutz); buttons (Memories in the Making); ribbon (Creative Impressions); distress ink (Ranger); postage stamp punch (EK Success); brads (ScrapArts); computer fonts (2P's White Sale, True Type); adhesives (Glue Dots International, Magic Scraps, Therm O Web)

DESTINY/PAGE 77

Patterned papers (Imagination Project); flowers (EK Success); die-cut photo turns, tag toppers (QuicKutz); brads (ScrapArts); computer font (2P's Peachy Keen); adhesives (Magic Scraps); cardstock; rickrack; staples

FOOTPRINTS ON THE MOON/PAGE 78

Textured cardstock (National Cardstock); circle punch (EK Success); brads (ScrapArts); dimensional foam squares (Therm O Web); computer font (Times New Roman); adhesive (Xyron)

DREAMS/PAGE 79

Patterned paper (Urban Lily); letter stickers (Sticker Studio); die-cut index tabs, photo turns (QuicKutz); acrylic charms (Heidi Grace Designs); rickrack (Memories in the Making); ribbon (May Arts); wire (Artistic Wire); letter stamps (PSX Design); solvent ink (Tsukineko); chalk ink (Clearsnap); brads (ScrapArts); computer font (AL Worn Machine); adhesives (Glue Dots International, Magic Scraps, Therm O Web); cardstock; staples; tags

BEGINNINGS OF ALL YOUR DREAMS/ PAGE 80

Patterned paper (Scenic Route Paper Co.); chipboard circles, monochromatic inks, brads, textured cardstock (Bazzill); photo turns (7 Gypsies); heart paper clip (Carolee's Creations); heart charm (Quest Beads); safety pin (Making Memories); metal photo corners (Scrapworks); scrapbook nails (Chatterbox); dimensional glaze (Ranger); adhesives (Glue Dots International, Magic Scraps, Therm O Web); computer font; jump ring; lace; ribbon; silk flowers

I MAKE PERFECT SENSE/PAGE 80

Lime cardstock (Collage Press); acrylic frame, chipboard flower, jewels (Heidi Swapp); ribbon (American Crafts, May Arts); wire (Artistic Wire); buttons (Memories in the Making); rub-on elements (7 Gypsies); chalk ink (Clearsnap); computer font (2P's Fabulous); adhesives (Glue Dots International, Magic Scraps, Stampin' Up!); charm; cardstock; safety pin; staples; twill tape

VERY LITTLE/PAGE 81

Chipboard monogram letter (Bazzill); patterned paper (Keeping Memories Alive); ribbons (American Crafts, May Arts); rickrack (Memories in the Making); clear buttons (7 Gypsies); wire (Artistic Wire); metal chain, flower, eyelets (Making Memories); brads (ScrapArts); chalk (Pebbles); chalk ink (Clearsnap); computer fonts (MA Fishy, MA Quaddie); adhesives (Magic Scraps, Therm O Web)

A JOURNEY/PAGE 81

Patterned papers (Autumn Leaves); chipboard, stamping ink (Bazzill); flourish stamps (Gel-a-Tins); velvet ribbon (Me & My Big Ideas); black trim (Venus Industries); chalk ink (Clearsnap); brads (Making Memories); computer font (Moonbeam Regular); adhesives (EK Success, Magic Scraps, Ross); jewelry findings

YOUR DREAMS/PAGE 82

Album (SEI); patterned papers, letter stickers (Chatterbox); chipboard letters (Heidi Swapp); chipboard flowers (Maya Road); buttons (Memories in the Making); chalk ink (Clearsnap); die-cut photo turns (QuicKutz); brads (ScrapArts); ribbons (May Arts, Me & My Big Ideas, Offray); twill (Creative Impressions); linen thread (Hillcreek Designs); computer font (Tiempo); adhesives (Glue Dots International, Magic Scraps, Ross, Xyron)

THERE WILL COME A TIME/PAGE 82

Patterned papers, distressed cardstock (Keeping Memories Alive); letter stamps (EK Success, Gel-a-Tins); distress ink (Ranger); solvent ink (Tsukineko); chipboard tiles (Bazzill); art hooks (Li'l Davis Designs); dye (Making Memories); jewelry tags, cotton lace (Fanny's Fabrics); paper flowers (Serendipity Designworks); brads (ScrapArts); computer font (Chelt Press); adhesives (Magic Scraps, Ross)

LIFE, MOMENTS, LOVE/PAGE 83

Textured cardstock, mini brads, monochromatic ink (Bazzill); sequin flowers, photo turns (Queen & Co.); die-cut letters, brackets (QuicKutz); colored brads (Making Memories); twill (Carolee's Creations); chalk ink (Clearsnap); adhesives (Therm O Web, Xyron); computer font (AL Old Remington); ribbon

ALEX'S GIFT/PAGE 84

Double-sided cardstock, patterned papers, moldings, nameplates, scrapbook tacks (Chatterbox); chipboard letters (Li'l Davis Designs); rub-on letters (Autumn Leaves, Chatterbox); die-cut index tab (Sizzix); paper flowers (Prima); photo turns (Q-T's); linen thread (Hillcreek Designs); button (Memories in the Making); chalk (Craf-T); monochromatic inks, textured cardstock (Bazzill); computer fonts (2P's Block Party, 2P's Renaissance); adhesives (Magic Scraps, Therm O Web); ribbon

LIVE FOREVER/PAGE 85

Patterned paper (EK Success); double-sided cardstock (Doodlebug Design); chipboard letters (Basic Grey); chalk ink (Clearsnap); rickrack (Memories in the Making); brads (ScrapArts); computer font (Inkster); adhesives (Magic Scraps, Therm O Web)

NONE OF US WILL EVER ACCOMPLISH/PAGE 86

Patterned paper (Scenic Route Paper Co., Scrapworks); mask (Heidi Swapp); rickrack (May Arts); heart clip (Q-T's); brads, photo turns (Making Memories); computer fonts (Harting, Mailart Rubberstamp, Script MT Bold); adhesive (EK Success); cardstock; stamping ink

WHISPER ALONE/PAGE 86

Patterned papers (Autumn Leaves); cardstock (Colorbök); letter stickers (Carolee's Creations); letter stamps (Gel-a-Tins); walnut ink crystals, photo turns, rub-ons (7 Gypsies); dimensional glaze, distress ink (Ranger); chalk ink (Clearsnap); solvent ink (Tsukineko); die-cut index tab (Sizzix); brads (ScrapArts); computer font (Colonial Dane); adhesive (Therm O Web); muslin; shipping tag

BARKERVILLE/PAGE 87

Patterned paper, key hole (7 Gypsies); chalk ink (Clearsnap); textured cardstock, brads (Bazzill); buttons, label holder (Making Memories); aged tag (Rusty Pickle); letter stickers (K & Company, Making Memories); ribbon (American Crafts); date stamp (Close To My Heart); embroidery floss (DMC); chipboard letters (Li'l Davis Designs); rub-ons (My Mind's Eye); texture paste (Delta); die-cut letters, index tab (QuicKutz); circle punch (EK Success); label maker (Dymo); adhesive (Tombow); computer fonts (Abadi MT Condensed Light, Bookman Old Style, 2Peas Ragtag, Lucida Sans Typewriter, CB Wednesday, CB Brush Strokes, Tw Cen MT Condensed); acrylic paint

NEW BEGINNINGS/PAGE 88

Walnut ink crystals, photo turns (7 Gypsies); walnut ink dauber (Fiber Scraps); walnut stain ink (Ranger); chalk ink (Clearsnap); letters, decorative brads, safety pins, stick pins, mini brads (Making Memories); tape measure twill tape (Carolee's Creations); cotton lace (Fanny's Fabrics); letter stamps (EK Success); date stamp (JustRite Stampers); computer font (P22 Typewriter); adhesives (EK Success, Magic Scraps); cardstock; charms; eyelet lace; flowers; shipping tags; twine

KNOW YOUR LIMITS/PAGE 88

Patterned paper (Urban Lily); textured cardstock (National Cardstock); twill tape (Carolee's Creations); ribbon (May Arts); die-cut flowers (QuicKutz); eyelets, brads (Making Memories); mini page pebbles (Memories in the Making); chalk ink (Clearsnap); computer font (2P's Fabulous); adhesives (EK Success, Magic Scraps, Therm O Web)

STEPH/PAGE 89

Scrapbook frame (Pageframe Designs); patterned papers, letter stickers (Collage Press); chipboard, brads (Bazzill); chalk ink (Clearsnap); rub-on letters, jewels (Me & My Big Ideas); photo turns (Making Memories); cotton lace (Fanny's Fabrics); computer font (Sharpie); adhesives (Glue Dots International, Magic Scraps); cardstock; flowers

ADORE/PAGE 90

Patterned papers (EK Success); epoxy letters (Li'l Davis Designs); clear letters (Heidi Swapp); paper flowers (Prima); chipboard hearts, photo turns (Making Memories); jewels (Me & My Big Ideas); die-cut index tabs (QuicKutz); monochromatic stamping ink (Bazzill); ribbons (May Arts, Textured Trios); rub-ons (Autumn Leaves); computer font (2P's Peachy Keen); adhesives (EK Success, Glue Dots International, Magic Scraps, Therm O Web, Xyron)

BE BRAVE/PAGE 90

Patterned papers (Junkitz); rub-on letters (Li'l Davis Designs); chipboard bookplate (Heidi Swapp); distress ink (Ranger); chalk ink (Clearsnap); die-cut photo turns, index tab (QuicKutz); brads (ScrapArts); transparency (Office Depot); computer fonts (Noveltease, P22 Typewriter); adhesives (Glue Dots International, Xyron); twine

DESTINY/PAGE 91

Patterned papers, scrapbook nails (Chatterbox); die-cut letters, photo turns (QuicKutz); clear flowers (Heidi Swapp); safety pins, mini eyelets, jump ring, paint (Making Memories); twill (Creative Imaginations); dimensional glaze (Ranger); computer font (AL Old Remington); adhesives (EK Success, Glue Dots International, Magic Scraps, Therm O Web, Xyron); twine

STRENGTH/PAGE 92

Patterned papers (Sweetwater); distress ink (Ranger); chalk ink (Clearsnap); mini page pebbles (Memories in the Making); die-cut photo turns (QuicKutz); brads (ScrapArts); computer fonts (2P's Evergreen, 2P's Tattered Lace); adhesives (Glue Dots International, Magic Scraps, Therm O Web); twine

SPREAD YOUR WINGS/PAGE 92

Patterned papers (My Mind's Eye); paper flowers (Prima); distress ink, dimensional glaze (Ranger); ribbon buckle (7 Gypsies); brads (ScrapArts); transparency (Office Depot); computer fonts (Lavishly Yours, P22 Petemoss); adhesives (EK Success, Glue Dots International, Magic Scraps, Xyron); buttons; charms; lace; ribbon

DREAMS/PAGE 93

Zippered mini album (Bazzill); rub-on border (Carolee's Creations); walnut ink, patterned paper (7 Gypsies); mica tiles (USArtQuest); paper glaze (Delta); distress ink, dimensional glaze (Ranger); solvent ink (Tsukineko); trim (Venus Industries); letter stamps (PSX Design); brads (Making Memories); circle punch (EK Success); adhesives (Glue Dots International, Magic Scraps); die-cut typewriter letters (source unknown); coarse salt; metal washers; shipping tag; twine

TO THE WORLD/PAGE 94

Patterned papers, tab and label stickers, letter stickers, brads, buttons (SEI); chalk ink (Clearsnap); textured cardstock (Bazzill); ribbon (Offray); letter stickers (Provo Craft); embroidery floss (DMC); die-cut photo turns (QuicKutz); circle punches (EK Success); photo corners (Heidi Swapp); computer font (Baskerville Old Face); adhesives (All Night Media, Tombow)

ONE PERSON/PAGE 94

Patterned papers (Junkitz); die-cut letters, index tabs, photo turns (QuicKutz); ribbon (May Arts); ribbon buckles (Memories in the Making); distress ink (Ranger); brads (ScrapArts); computer font (Mayflower); adhesives (EK Success, Xyron)

ONE WORLD/PAGE 95

Patterned paper (7 Gypsies, Scenic Route Paper Co., Scrapworks); chipboard letters, brads, photo turns (Making Memories); clay letter tiles (Li'l Davis Designs); label stamps (FontWerks); acrylic paint (Heidi Swapp); textured paint (Delta); metallic rub-ons (Craf-T); distress ink (Ranger); textured cardstock (Bazzill); chipboard; thread

Source guide

The following companies manufacture products featured in this book. Please check your local retailers to find these materials, or go to a company's Web site for the latest product. In addition, we have made every attempt to properly credit the items mentioned in this book. We apologize to any company that we have listed incorrectly, and we would appreciate hearing from you.

7 Gypsies
(877) 749-7797
www.sevengypsies.com

AccuCut®
(800) 288-1670
www.accucut.com

Activa® Products, Inc.
(800) 883-3899
www.activaproducts.com

Aleen's-no contact info

All My Memories
(888) 553-1998
www.allmymemories.com

All Night Media
(see Plaid Enterprises)

American Crafts
(801) 226-0747
www.americancrafts.com

Artistic Wire
(630) 530-7567
www.artisticwire.com

Autumn Leaves
(800) 588-6707
www.autumnleaves.com

Basic Grey™
(801) 451-6006
www.basicgrey.com

Bazzill Basics Paper
(480) 558-8557
www.bazzillbasics.com

Berwick Offray™, LLC
(800) 344-5533
www.offray.com

Blue Moon Beads
(800) 377-6715
www.bluemoonbeads.com

Bo-Bunny Press
(801) 771-4010
www.bobunny.com

Carolee's Creations®
(435) 563-1100
www.ccpaper.com

Chatterbox, Inc.
(208) 939-9133
www.chatterboxinc.com

Clearsnap, Inc.
(360) 293-6634
www.clearsnap.com

Close To My Heart®
(888) 655-6552
www.closetomyheart.com

Collage Press
(435) 656-4611
www.collagepress.com

Colorbök™, Inc.
(800) 366-4660
www.colorbok.com

Craf-T Products
(507) 235-3996
www.craf-tproducts.com

Creative Imaginations
(800) 942-6487
www.cigift.com

Creative Impressions Rubber Stamps, Inc.
(719) 596-4860
www.creativeimpressions.com

Creative Memories®
(800) 468-9335
www.creativememories.com

Daisy D's Paper Company
(888) 601-8955
www.daisydspaper.com

Dèjá Views
(800) 243-8419
www.dejaviews.com

Delta Technical Coatings, Inc.
(800) 423-4135
www.deltacrafts.com

DMC Corp.
(973) 589-0606
www.dmc.com

Doodlebug Design™ Inc.
(801) 966-9952
www.doodlebug.ws

Duncan Enterprises
(800) 782-6748
www.duncan-enterprises .com

Dymo
(800) 426-7827
www.dymo.com

EK Success™, Ltd.
(800) 524-1349
www.eksuccess.com

Emagination Crafts, Inc.
(866) 238-9770
www.emaginationcrafts.com

Esselte Corporation
http://corporate.esselte.com

Fanny's Fabrics-no contact info

Fiber Scraps™
(215) 230-4905
www.fiberscraps.com

Fiskars®, Inc.
(800) 950-0203
www.fiskars.com

FontWerks
(604) 942-3105
www.fontwerks.com

Gel-a-Tins
(800) 393-2151
www.gelatinstamps.com

Global Solutions
(206) 343-5210
www.globalsolutionsonline.com

Glue Dots® International
(888) 688-7131
www.gluedots.com

Go West Studios
(214) 227-0007
www.goweststudios.com

Heidi Grace Designs, Inc.
(608) 294-4509
www.heidigrace.com

Heidi Swapp/Advantus Corporation
(904) 482-0092
www.heidiswapp.com

Herma- no contact info

Hero Arts® Rubber Stamps, Inc.
(800) 822-4376
www.heroarts.com

Hillcreek Designs
(619) 562-5799
www.hillcreekdesigns.com

Homemade Memories
www.myhomemadememories.com

Imagination Project, Inc.
(513) 860-2711
www.imaginationproject.com

Jesse James & Co., Inc.
(610) 435-0201
www.jessejamesbutton.com

JewelCraft, LLC
(201) 223-0804
www.jewelcraft.biz

Junkitz™
(732) 792-1108
www.junkitz.com

JustRite® Stampers/
Millenium Marking Company
(847) 806-1750
www.justritestampers.com

K & Company
(888) 244-2083
www.kandcompany.com

Karen Foster Design
(801) 451-9779
www.karenfosterdesign.com

Keeping Memories Alive™
(800) 419-4949
www.scrapbooks.com

KI Memories
(972) 243-5595
www.kimemories.com

Krylon®
(216) 566-200
www.krylon.com

Lara's Crafts
(800) 232-5272
www.larascrafts.com

Li'l Davis Designs
(949) 838-0344
www.lildavisdesigns.com

Magenta Rubber Stamps
(800) 565-5254
www.magentastyle.com

Magic Scraps™
(972) 238-1838
www.magicscraps.com

Making Memories
(800) 286-5263
www.makingmemories.com

Ma Vinci's Reliquary
http://crafts.dm.net/
mall/reliquary/

Maya Road, LLC
(214) 488-3279
www.mayaroad.com

May Arts
(800) 442-3950
www.mayarts.com

McGill, Inc.
(800) 982-9884
www.mcgillinc.com

me & my BiG ideas®
(949) 883-2065
www.meandmybigideas.com

Melissa Frances/Heart & Home, Inc.
(905) 686-9031
www.melissafrances.com

Memories in the Making
(604) 850-8562
www.memoriesembellishments.com

Michaels® Arts & Crafts
(800) 642-4235
www.michaels.com

My Mind's Eye™, Inc.
(800) 665-5116
www.frame-ups.com

My Sentiments Exactly
(719) 260-6001
www.sentiments.com

National Cardstock- no longer in business

Nunn Design
(360) 379-3557
www.nunndesign.com

Office Depot
www.officedepot.com

Offray- see Berwick Offray, LLC

Once Upon A Charm...
(866) 6CHARMS
www.onceuponacharm.com

Pageframe Designs
(877) 55frame
www.scrapbookframe.com

Paper Adventures®
(800) 525-3196
www.paperadventures.com

Paper Heart Studio
(904) 230-8108
www.paperheartstudio.com

Pebbles Inc.
(801) 224-1857
www.pebblesinc.com

Plaid Enterprises, Inc.
(800) 842-4197
www.plaidonline.com

Polyform Products Co.
(847) 427-0020
www.sculpey.com

Pressed Petals
(800) 748-4656
www.pressedpetals.com

Prima Marketing, Inc.
(909) 627-5532
www.mulberrypaperflowers.com

Provo Craft®
(888) 577-3545
www.provocraft.com

PSX Design™
(800) 782-6748
www.psxdesign.com

Q-T's- no contact info

Queen & Co.
(858) 485-5132
www.queenandco.com

Quest Beads & Cast, Inc.
(212) 354-0979
www.questbeads.com

QuicKutz, Inc.
(801) 765-1144
www.quickutz.com

Ranger Industries, Inc.
(800) 244-2211
www.rangerink.com

Reminisce Papers
(319) 358-9777
www.shopreminisce.com

River City Rubber Works
(877) 735-2276
www.rivercityrubberworks.com

Ross- no contact info

Rubber Stampede
(800) 423-4135
www.deltacrafts.com

Rusty Pickle
(801) 746-1045
www.rustypickle.com

Sandylion Sticker Designs
(800) 387-4215
www.sandylion.com

Scenic Route Paper Co.
(801) 785-0761
www.scenicroutepaper.com

ScrapArts
(503) 631-4893
www.scraparts.com

Scrapbook Wizard™, The
(435) 752-7555
www.scrapbookwizard.com

Scrappin' Extras™/Punch Crazy
Scrapbooking
(403) 271-9649
www.scrappinextras.com

Scraptivity™ Scrapbooking, Inc.
(800) 393-2151
www.scraptivity.com

Scrapworks, LLC
(801) 363-1010
www.scrapworks.com

SEI, Inc.
(800) 333-3279
www.shopsei.com

Serendipity Designworks
(250) 743-7642
www.serendipitydesignworks.com

Sheer Creations- no contact info

Sizzix®
(866) 742-4447
www.sizzix.com

Stampin' Up!®
(800) 782-6787
www.stampinup.com

Stewart Superior Corporation
(800) 558-2875
www.stewartsuperior.com

Sticker Studio™
(208) 322-2465
www.stickerstudio.com

Sweetwater
(800) 359-3094
www.sweetwaterscrapbook.com

Textured Trios- no contact info

Therm O Web, Inc.
(800) 323-0799
www.thermoweb.com

Tombow®
(800) 835-3232
www.tombowusa.com

Tsukineko®, Inc.
(800) 769-6633
www.tsukineko.com

Urban Lily- no contact info

USArtQuest, Inc.
(517) 522-6225
www.usartquest.com

U.S. Shell, Inc.
(956) 943-1709
www.usshell.com

Venus Industries
(800) 221-6097
www.venusindustries.com

Wimpole Street Creations
(801) 298-0504
www.wimpolestreet.com

Wordsworth
(719) 282-3495
www.wordsworthstamps.com

Xyron
(800) 793-3523
www.xyron.com

Yarn Collection, The
(415) 383-9276
fibergoddess@msn.com

Karen Cobb enjoys scrapbooking as it gives her the opportunity to be expressive through creative art that will always be cherished by her family. Her work has been published in various books and magazines, and she has designed scrapbook art for manufacturers and Web sites. When she is not scrapbooking, you will find her gardening, walking the dog, admiring the ocean view or spending time with her three teenage daughters, Tiffany, Aleisha, and Kristina, and her husband, Chris. Karen currently lives in Victoria, British Columbia.

Sandra Ash was first introduced to scrapbooking five years ago. Her goal was to find a hobby to share with her daughter and to organize her family photos. She loves the creative outlet scrapbooking provides. Sandra's handwriting has been turned into a popular line of letter stamps, letter stickers and rub-ons by Carolee's Creations. Her work has been seen in various scrapbooking publications, and she is on several design teams. Along with scrapbooking, Sandra enjoys reading, knitting and sewing. She lives in Victoria, British Columbia with her husband Mike and their three children, Taylor, Jake and Annie.

As a member of a creative family, Trudy's interest in art started at an early age and continued to grow throughout her school years and into college where she studied graphic and fine arts. But it wasn't until years later in November 2000 after she became an avid rubber stamper that Trudy first walked into a scrapbook store—and her new addiction for the art of scrapbooking began. Since being selected as one of the original Memory Makers Masters in 2003, she has become a regular artwork contributor to *Memory Makers* magazine and books. Her achievements include designing the cover art for the 2004 Layout Mania special issue and being featured in the October 2004 *Memory Makers* article appropriately titled "Truly Trudy."

After teaching and demonstrating for different manufacturers at U.S. and Canadian trade shows, Trudy has gained popularity amongst the teaching circuit and has taught at Camp Memory Makers for two years as well as on one of Memory Makers' Caribbean Croppin' Cruises. She can still be found teaching at scrapbook conventions and as a guest instructor at scrapbook stores in North America. Trudy and her artwork have also made numerous television appearances, and much of her work has been featured by *Memory Makers* founder Michele Gerbrandt on "Scrapbook Memories." In 2004, Trudy also made several guest appearances on the "DIY Scrapbooking" show with host Sandi Genovese.

Originally from England, Trudy now lives in Victoria on Vancouver Island in British Columbia, Canada, with her children and scrapbooking inspirations, Aysha and Alex, and their furry, four-legged companions Tia and Moggie.

Index

12 x 12 (31 cm x 31 cm) scrapbook pages, 1, 14, 16, 19, 20, 23-24, 27-28, 30, 32-33, 37, 39-41, 43, 44-45, 47, 53-54, 58, 60-61, 63, 68, 70-71, 73, 76, 79-80, 83-84, 87, 88, 90, 92, 95

8.5 x 11 (21.6 cm x 27.9 cm) scrapbook pages, 12, 34, 56, 74

Acrylic, 21-22, 24, 44-45, 51-55, 60, 67, 69, 74, 79-80, 89-91

Adversity, overcoming, 88

Albums, 21, 38, 48, 82, 93

Alcohol inks, 23, 74

Ash, Sandra, 23, 25, 42, 55, 62, 73, 86, 95

Author & contributing artists' biographies, 110

Autumn, 70-71

Beach, 62-63

Black-and-white photos, 24, 30, 33, 37, 40-41, 45, 74, 88-90, 92

Chapter 1, Love, 12-33

Chapter 2, Cherish, 34-55

Chapter 3, Discover, 56-73

Chapter 4, Imagine, 74-95

Children, 1, 16-26, 40-43

Chipboard, 8, 12, 14, 16-18, 21, 24, 27, 30-32, 34, 38-41, 44-48, 50-51, 55, 60, 63-64, 67, 69, 72-74, 80-82, 84-85, 87, 89-90, 95

Clay, 73, 95

Cobb, Karen, 22, 24, 42, 55, 63, 72, 87, 94

Dedication, 3

Destiny, 91

Dimensional glaze, 12, 15, 24, 29, 32, 34, 39-41, 46, 50, 56, 59-60, 69, 74, 86, 91

Dreams, 8, 79

Fabric, 17, 38-39, 42, 50, 58, 62-64, 86, 88

Family, 6, 12-33

Fibers, 21, 30

Friendship, 34, 44-49

Grandparents, 12, 30-32

Handcut lettering, 16-17, 28, 30, 40-43, 46, 54, 60, 62-64, 67, 70, 76, 78, 88, 92

Happiness, 84

Heritage, 28-30

Horizontal borders, 17, 31, 39, 46, 68, 71, 85, 88

Incorporating poems, quotes and sayings, 8-11

Introduction, 6-7

Machine-stitching, 12, 17, 22, 27, 32, 34, 39, 41-46, 49-53, 59-62, 66-67, 70-71, 79-80, 83, 85, 88, 90-92, 94-95

Masking, 48, 86

Metallic flakes, 69

Monograms, 44, 64, 72, 81-82, 85

Multiple-photo layouts, 19, 32, 40-41, 53, 60-61, 65, 70-71, 73, 79-80, 84, 87, 90, 95

Nature, 58-59, 72-73

New beginnings, 88

Organic shapes, 25, 40, 55, 59, 72

Parents, 27

Pets, 50-55

Quote variations, 22-25, 42-43, 54-55, 62-63, 86-87, 94-95

Quotes, where to find them, 9

Scrapbook wall art, 89

Sepia photos, 27

Single-photo layouts, 12, 14, 16, 20, 23-24, 27-28, 30, 33-34, 37, 39, 41, 43-45, 47, 54, 56, 58, 60, 63, 68, 74, 76, 88-89, 92

Sketches, 96-102

Sketching out a design, 10-11

Slide mounts, 23

Source Guide, 108-109

Spouse, 37, 39

Spring, 64-67

Stamping, 8, 15, 17, 20-22, 24-26, 28-30, 32-33, 37, 39-40, 44-46, 50, 54-55, 59, 62, 68-69, 71, 73, 79, 82, 86, 88, 93, 95

Step-by-step instructions, 15, 23-24, 26, 30, 38, 43, 48, 50, 54, 58, 63, 69, 73, 76, 87, 89, 91, 93, 95

Summer, 68-69

Supply Lists, 103-107

Table of Contents, 4-5

Tags, 17, 18, 51, 52, 66, 81

Texture paste, 87, 95

Travel, 14, 76

Tribute, 30, 33, 92

Vertical borders, 6, 8, 14-15, 21-22, 25-26, 29, 36, 40, 42, 44, 46, 49-50, 55, 59, 61-62, 64, 67, 69-70, 72, 77-78, 82, 86, 91-92, 94

Winter, 56, 60-61

Learn more amazing techniques from the authors of these inspiring Memory Makers Books.

A Passion for Specialty Paper
Brandi Ginn & Pam Klassen
ISBN-13: 978-1-892127-61-7
ISBN-10: 1-892127-61-X
paperback, 96 pgs., #33460

Creative Collage for Scrapbooks
Kelly Angard
ISBN-13: 978-1-892127-58-7
ISBN-10: 1-892127-58-X
paperback, 128 pgs., #33419

Scrapbook Memorabilia
Cori Dahmen
ISBN-13: 978-1-892127-76-1
ISBN-10: 1-892127-76-8
paperback, 96 pgs., #Z0011

A Passion for Patterned Paper
Brandi Ginn & Pam Klassen
ISBN-13: 978-1-892127-51-8
ISBN-10: 1-892127-51-2
paperback, 96 pgs., #33265

Creative Painting for Scrapbookers
Lori Bergmann
ISBN-13: 978-1-892127-66-2
ISBN-10: 1-892127-66-0
paperback, 96 pgs., #33463

These books and other fine Memory Makers Books titles are available from your local art or craft retailer, bookstore or on-line supplier. Please see page 2 of this book for contact information for Canada, Australia, the U.K. and Europe.